Love and Logic Magic for Early
Childhood
Practical Parenting from Birth to Six Years

— SECOND EDITION —

Love and Logic

2207 Jackson Street, Golden, CO 80401
800-338-4065 • www.loveandlogic.com

Jim Fay & Charles Fay, Ph.D.

Love and Logic Institute, Inc.
2207 Jackson Street
Golden, CO 80401
800-338-4065
www.loveandlogic.com

Love and Logic, Love & Logic, Becoming a Love and Logic Parent, America's Parenting Experts, Love and Logic Magic, 9 Essential Skills for the Love and Logic Classroom, Love and Logic Early Childhood Parenting Made Fun!, Early Childhood Parenting Made Fun!, Parenting the Love and Logic Way, and 🔒 are registered trademarks or trademarks of the Institute For Professional Development, Ltd. and may not be used without written permission expressly granted from the Institute For Professional Development, Ltd.

ISBN# 978-1-942105-14-5

Library of Congress Control number: 00-101452

Publication Coordinator: Charles Fay, Ph.D., Golden, CO
Second Edition Copyediting: Joyce M. Gilmour, Brooklyn, WI
Second Edition Typesetting: Michael C. Snell, Lawrence, KS

Published and printed in the United States of America.

Table of Contents

Also authored by Jim Fay
- Parents are not ATM's
- Preventing Teen Rebellion
- Parenting with Love and Logic
- Love and Logic Magic When Kids Drain Your Energy
- Toddlers and Pre-Schoolers

Also authored by Charles Fay, Ph.D.
- Painless Parenting for the Preschool Years II
- Stepparenting with Love and Logic
- Technology and Kids
- Real Talk on Technology
- Love and Logic Keys to Helping Kids Cope with Divorce

Multimedia training curricula by Love and Logic Institute, Inc.
- Parenting the Love and Logic Way®
- Love and Logic Early Childhood Parenting Made Fun!®
- 9 Essential Skills for the Love and Logic Classroom®

Call us today to find the right Love and Logic
solution-geared product for you!
1-800-338-4065
Or visit our website:
www.loveandlogic.com

Raises Responsible Kids • Easy to Learn • Changes Lives • You Can Start Using It Right Away

Acknowledgments

Mom, Dad, and all of you wonderful Love and Logic parents

As it's often said, "Time flies when you're havin' fun." Years have passed since we published the first edition of this book, and we've been having more fun than two toddlers with toothpaste and no parental supervision. Much of it has to do with the wonderful comments and questions we get from parents using the Love and Logic approach.

Interestingly, one of the most common questions is, "Were you really raised with Love and Logic?"

I often joke, "Yep. That's why I became a child psychologist… just to figure out what happened to me as a kid!"

The truth be told, my parents, Jim and Shirley Fay, weren't always into this stuff. Until I was about eight, they only had two parenting skills: One apiece. My father's strategy involved yelling, "For crying out loud!" My mother's was to softly threaten, "If yooooooou keep acting that way…gypsies will come."

Needless to say, the gradual development of Love and Logic was a godsend to our family. Over the years, my mom and dad gradually moved from using anger, lectures, and threats to becoming some of the most unconditionally loving and calm parents on the planet. As I watched their transformation, I became more and more intrigued by this very strange yet wonderful combination of love and logic. As an adult, I'm thankful every day for their encouragement and unconditional love. I'm also thankful that they allowed me to make mistakes and to experience the logical or natural consequences. They grew to understand that small mistakes made early in life are far more affordable learning experiences than large ones made later on.

Thanks, Mom and Dad!

Thanks also to all of the wonderful parents who've contributed to our growing understanding of how to parent little ones. Your wonderful feedback and suggestions have made creating this second edition a joy.

Jim, Foster, and Little Charlie

Cancun, Mexico, 1978. Dr. Foster Cline and I sat in the cabana on the beach. Foster was and still is my very best friend, loyal partner, and personal guru. We had guided one hundred twenty teachers and parents to the resort for three weeks of fun and study. Most of the participants were rollicking in the surf while Foster and I were chasing our passion. The flame behind that passion, known as Love and Logic®, has not dwindled one bit over the years that have passed since that day.

Foster and I were designing yet another lesson for our students. The energy was evident as we threw ideas at each other at warp speed. This is what happens every time we get together.

"We have to make this even more practical and easier to master than the last lesson," enthused Foster. "That way they'll remember the technique and use it as soon as they see their kids again."

Make it simple. Make it easy to remember. And best of all, make it practical. Those have been the watchwords of our teaching from day one. Over the years these principles have not only attracted millions to study Love and Logic, but have captured Foster's and my imagination and energy.

Little did we know, on that day, a fourteen-year-old boy was watching us. This boy was Charlie Fay, my son. He was curious about why his dad and Foster had so much fun working together. Not only was he curious, he was determined to find out. So this was not the only time that he stayed close and eavesdropped on our every word. This is why he often appeared in the back of the classroom when Foster and I were teaching together.

It was years later that Charlie explained to us why he had studied to become a psychologist. "I watched the two of you share the joys of your friendship and teaching. I watched your enthusiasm as your first books and training programs became realities. I came to realize that what you did was not work. It was play. It was a passion. It was never a job."

Charlie continued, "Dad, I watched you and Mom setting up businesses. You worked together at the dining room table, licking stamps, making flyers, helping parents and teachers on the phone, counting advertising pieces, and stapling books. Even that wasn't a job for you. It was a passion.

"I decided that when I grew up I was going to be part of your dream to make Love and Logic a household word. I just never let you know it."

Once I heard Charlie talk about this I knew why he had become such an outstanding psychologist, writer, and speaker. Not only had he earned a Ph.D. in school psychology, but he had been studying Love and Logic with Foster and me since he was a child.

As we write this second edition, we often reflect on how thankful we are for each other. Having a successful son is nice. Having a loving and kind one is even better. Having a great relationship later in life with a loving and kind son is great beyond imagination.

Now that I'm in my forties (times two) I often reflect on the lessons I've learned about parenting. While the world is a vastly different place than it was only fifteen years ago, children still need the same things: Loving limits, plenty of opportunities to make decisions, the luxury of making mistakes early in life, and parents who love them enough to hold them accountable with empathy instead of anger.

Since we published the first edition of *Love and Logic Magic for Early Childhood*, we've been amazed by the demand for this book. Much of this has to do with the creativity and exceptional writing skills of Dr. Charles Fay, my son. I was proud to contribute to the first edition. Now I've been given the gift of helping with the second.

More than ever, I'm excited to offer more creative Love and Logic solutions for parents of young children. *Love and Logic Magic for Early Childhood* (Second Edition) is sure to be a winner.

Have fun with your kids. Remember that the loving relationships you're building now will be the ones that bring you immeasurable comfort when you're forty times two.

Jim Fay

Preface

We've included QR codes within the text of this book. When you scan these codes you will hear additional commentary and soundbites on a subject or thought (noted with the audio icon). We hope you find these helpful as you learn how to implement Love and Logic skills with your little ones.

How would it be if you could giggle your way through a book and also gain time-tested, powerful tools for raising happy, responsible kids? Wouldn't it be great if this very same book had so many fun techniques and examples that it actually started making you look forward to your young children misbehaving? Wouldn't it be wonderful if these very same tools and techniques could lower your stress level during these challenging years? These were the questions we asked as we introduced the first edition of this book. Today, even more than then, we're dedicated to helping parents enjoy the earliest years with their children. Now, even more than fifteen years ago, we understand that the more fun parents have with their tots, the better relationships they'll enjoy when those tots become teens.

Relationships are the key!

The last few years have taught us a great deal about the importance of loving connections…and that children are far more likely to develop good character and responsibility when they know that we adore them beyond words. How would it be…

then…if the skills in this book allowed you to discipline your children without losing their love and respect? What if we could show you how to set limits and provide effective consequences without creating resentment or rebellion?

During the years 1999-2000, as we planned the first edition of this book, the two of us spent hours brainstorming what to include. "Let's make this book really fun to read with lots of practical examples," I (Charles) said to my dad.

"Great! And let's be sure to give a bunch of solutions for really common problems people have with their young children… frustrating things they deal with each and every day," he replied.

What problems are the most typical and challenging for parents of young children? Our list in 2000 read something like this:

- Grocery store temper tantrums
- Bedtime battles
- Power struggles over eating
- Getting children to brush their teeth
- Potty training
- Whining and saying things like, "Not fair!" or, "But why?"
- Kids who won't get ready on time in the mornings
- Sibling rivalry
- Getting kids to pick up their toys
- Temper tantrums and fits in restaurants
- When they say, "No!" all of the time
- Begging for toys or candy in the checkout line
- Misbehaving at daycare, preschool, or kindergarten

As you can see, all of these concerns are completely outdated. Obviously we're just kidding! For some odd reason, parents of little ones are still challenged by these age-old struggles. Making parenting even more demanding, many of today's parents are grappling with:

- Meltdowns over wanting to use Mommy's smartphone, tablet, or laptop.
- How to set and enforce limits over screens.

- Frustration and power struggles having to do with increased learning demands placed on young children by many schools.
- Increasing pressure to "keep up with the Joneses" by raising perfect children.

As we planned the first edition of this book, we became more and more excited about the wonderful opportunities provided when little ones act up. As we completed this second edition, we became even more enthused. Why are we still so thrilled about young children and their misbehavior?

First, our enthusiasm grows daily as we continue to hear success story after success story describing how parents of young children are using Love and Logic to bring the fun back into parenting.

Second, research and real-world experience continues to remind us of how important it is that young children and their parents get off to a positive start. When parents begin using Love and Logic early in their children's lives, they often remark, "I didn't think parenting could be this much fun!" When parents wait too long to start, they often lament, "I wish I had started this stuff a whole lot earlier. Now things are really a battle."

Third, we love it when kids misbehave and make mistakes around Love and Logic adults. Why? Because Love and Logic teaches how to turn every mistake your children make into golden nuggets of wisdom. The more mistakes your children make, the wiser they become. As our world becomes faster paced and more temptation laden, does it become even more important that our children gain this wisdom before they enter it?

Lastly, we've come to realize that every time our children act up, and we provide consequences with empathy rather than anger, it allows them to see how much we love 'em. Think about it. When do we most deeply experience how much we are loved? Is it mostly when we're doing all the right things? Or is it more so when we are acting not so lovely yet continue to receive love?

Are you ready to have some fun?
If so, read on!

About the Authors

JIM FAY'S background includes thirty-one years as a teacher and administrator, twenty-four years as a professional consultant and public speaker, and many years as a parent of three children.

He serves both nationally and internationally as a consultant to schools, parent organizations, counselors, mental health organizations, and the U.S. military.

Jim believes his major accomplishment in life is the development (along with Foster W. Cline, M.D.) of a unique philosophy of practical techniques for enhancing communication between children and adults, known as Love and Logic. Jim has taken complex problems and broken them down into simple, easy-to-use concepts and techniques that can be understood and used by anyone. Hundreds of thousands of people have expressed how Love and Logic has enhanced their relationships with their children.

Jim is one of America's most sought-after presenters in the area of parenting and school discipline. His practical techniques are revolutionizing the way parents and professionals are looking at how we deal with children; how we help them become responsible, thinking people; and how we help them build a healthy sense of self.

CHARLES FAY, Ph.D. is a parent, author, and consultant to schools, parent groups, and mental health professionals around the world. His expertise in developing and teaching practical discipline strategies has been refined through work with severely disturbed youth in school, hospital, and community settings. Charles has developed an acute understanding of the most challenging students. Having grown up with Love and Logic, he also provides a unique...and often humorous...perspective.

CHAPTER ONE

Basic Ingredients of Love and Logic Magic

Parenting Can Still Be a Joy!

Imagine yourself enjoying a wonderful after-dinner conversation with family and friends. Life is good, because the meal went well, even with your toddler in attendance. You're amazed she actually swallowed the food she placed in her mouth. You're extremely thankful that nothing was thrown.

Like an angel, she smiles at you and asks, "Me play games?"

You reply lovingly, "No, sweetie. No games on Mommy's tablet."

The rest of the group suddenly stops conversing and glances your way. You know what they are thinking, "Let's see if that latest parenting book is actually working."

In your heart, you want to believe that a child—this child— can learn to listen the first time. In your soul, you desperately want to believe this stuff called Love and Logic® will really work. The pressure is on, and your little one knows it. Smiling in a not-so-angelic way, she begins to meander toward your nearby tablet.

You decide to try what you read in the book. You smile at her and sing, "Uh-oh. Uh-oh." You pick her up, bring her over and hold her lovingly in your lap. Following the book's instructions, you also keep the words to a minimum, you keep your mouth shut.

She is definitely not thanking you for your new parenting skills. The drama has hit academy award proportions as she cries, whines, and screams, "Mommy! You not my friend!"

Doing a little acting of your own, you smile and empathetically reply, "Oh, this is so sad. I will let you down when you are acting sweet."

She throws an even bigger fit. Your brother—whose kids play four to six hours of video games daily—says, "What's the big deal? She's just a little kid."

You politely smile and ask him if he also needs to be held until he can act sweet. There's a moment of awkward silence, then someone changes the subject. Everyone tries their best to ignore what's going on in your lap, and you begin to silently pray.

After a few minutes, your little sweetie is no longer whining or crying. "Maybe it will work!" you say to yourself. Now that she's calm, you give her a loving kiss and release her. Free at last, she heads straight back toward the tablet. All conversation stops, and your guests' mouths hang open.

She looks at the tablet, back at you, then at the tablet, then back at you. "Uh-oh," you sing once more. Finally, she points to the forbidden device, smiles and sings, "Uh-oh. No games!" Then, to everyone's amazement she runs to you, jumps in your lap, and hugs you tightly.

Oh, the love and confidence you see in her. This, you tell yourself, is how happy kids are when they have the security of having limits and parents who are able to enforce these limits in loving ways.

❤ ❤ ❤

Wouldn't it be great if you could sing "Uh-oh" to your children—just two syllables—and, like this wonderful little girl, they would stop in their tracks? Would you consider it a miracle, if, with a single phrase like "Uh-oh," your children would mind you? Wouldn't it be great if you never again had to raise your voice in frustration and anger?

You're thinking, yes, yes, yes, in answer to all these questions and wondering what on earth you have to do to make the dream come true. We're not going to tell you to love your kids more. You've already proven that you love them by taking the time to read this book. What we will do is give you some practical strategies for raising them without raising your blood pressure.

With Love and Logic, you will learn how to discipline your kids without losing their love and respect. They will learn to make choices that lead to happy and responsible lives. ◀》

What you're about to read requires an investment—of time and practice—but it will repay you and your children for years and generations to come.

Increasing the Odds

The story you just read about the toddler and the tablet is not a fairytale. It really did happen, and it can happen in your house, too. For more than thirty-five years, parents have been telling us: "It really works! Love and Logic ideas are easy. They're also so much fun that I actually look forward to my kids misbehaving, so I can use them!"

There are never any guarantees in parenting. Raising kids is tougher than ever, and there are many factors that fall beyond our control. Before I (Charles) became a parent, I believed kids would always turn out great if their parents simply used the correct skills. One of the many wonderful things about children is how they serve to humble us. As we have aged—and hopefully matured—we've come to recognize that good parenting is all about raising the odds and consistently doing the best we can.

Fortunately, nobody is perfect. Fortunately, we don't have to be. As you read the pages of this book, I (Jim) hope that you'll take some advice from a guy who's worked with families for roughly six decades:

Be patient with yourself. Don't be afraid to make some mistakes.

Don't expect yourself to be perfect, and don't expect your kids to be either.

Enjoy the ride.

While there are no absolute guarantees in parenting, Love and Logic can promise to dramatically raise the odds and allow you to look back years from now with no regrets. We're excited about this book. We believe that by using its principles now—when your children are young—you will make a great investment in their future.

Investing in the Future

People who move from one day to the next, without thinking about the days and years to come, wind up unprepared for the future. Remember the story, "The Grasshopper and the Ant"?

> One winter day, an ant was busy working with its fellow ants to dry their stored supply of corn, which had gotten damp during a rainstorm. A grasshopper approached and begged the ant to spare her a few grains. "I'm starving," the grasshopper said.
>
> Even though it was against his principles to stop working, one ant stopped for a moment and asked, "May I ask what you were doing all last spring and summer? Why didn't you collect a store of food for the winter?"
>
> "The fact is," replied the grasshopper, "I was busy singing. I didn't have time."
>
> "If you spent the summer singing," said the ant,

"you're going to have to spend the winter dancing." And he went back to work.

❤ ❤ ❤

Not a very charitable ant? Perhaps. But he was right to question the grasshopper's failure to think about his future. Do you suppose it's wise to invest early, in the "spring" of our children's lives, so that we don't have to spend the winter dancing around teenagers who are out of control? We are guessing you already know this. That's why you're reading this book.

Let's take a look at Emma, a fifteen-year-old whose parents— unlike you—didn't start early:

> "I can't believe you expect me to use this old phone. It doesn't do anything," Emma griped to her mother.
>
> "Do you think that money grows on trees? That's the one you're getting, and I'm not buying you another!"
>
> "You never loved me!" screamed Emma. "If you loved me, you'd buy me a new one. This is so old it probably won't even work if there's an emergency! I guess you just want me to die somewhere because I can't get help."
>
> Burned by guilt, Mom caves. "It's just that you don't understand how expensive things are. Okay—I'll buy you this one, but you better take better care of it than the last one you lost!"

❤ ❤ ❤

Now, let's look at what you can look forward to by investing early:

> "This old phone of mine is pretty embarrassing," Noah said to his mother.
>
> Mom answered, "Yeah, I guess a lot of kids have the latest thing."
>
> Noah smiled. "The new Me-Phone 7 is only five hundred dollars. You could buy me one."

"That's right," Mom replied, "and when do you think that will happen?" ◄»

"Uh—like when the Me-Phone 2000 comes out when I'm eighty."

Patting him on the back, Mom joked, "Think how affordable the 7 version will be by then. You'll probably be able to get one for ten bucks. I love you."

"Yeah, I guess I love you, too, even though I am the only kid with an antique phone."

❤ ❤ ❤

Noah's mother started early, making deposits into her parenting account. While he's not a perfect kid, he's generally fun to be around, basically responsible, and understands that his parents are not his slaves.

We thank you for starting early. Down the road, there will be many other people who'll thank you, too—your child's teachers, friends, loved ones—and, sooner or later—your child.

Four Types of Deposits:
The Basic Principles of Love and Logic

As we are well into the 21st century, are children ingesting far more information than we did at their age? Is some of this information positive and healthy? Is some of it, by contrast, scary? Clearly, kids are facing far more serious—sometimes life-and-death—decisions than ever before. Many of these are piped directly into their little hands via the internet. Are they going to need more wisdom than we did, just to survive? Where are they going to get this wisdom? Here's the good news:

Regardless of all our technological advances, parents will always be the most important source of information and values for their growing children.

How can parents provide this essential information? By using the four basic Love and Logic ingredients. What do these ingredients offer? They give parents a practical investment strategy for building their children's confidence, personal responsibility, and ability to make smart choices. Wise people like you start early in their children's lives, making four types of deposits. Through their everyday lives with their children, they try their best to:

- Help them develop a healthy sense of self.
- Share the control or decision making.
- Offer empathy, then consequences.
- Share the thinking and problem solving.

PRINCIPLE #1: *Guide them toward a healthy sense of self*

In the first edition of this book, Principle #1 read, "Build the Self-Concept." Since that time, we've become more and more concerned about using this terminology. Why so? The term "self-concept" is used too frequently to imply that parents should ensure that their children are always happy and feel good about themselves. While we want this, too, we understand that sometimes we must allow our kids to learn about life by experiencing disappointments and struggles.

Sometimes we must allow our kids to learn about life by experiencing disappointments and struggles.

In today's world, too many adults believe that the universe revolves around them and that everything should be easy. Because they were constantly praised and rewarded by their well-meaning parents and teachers, they now believe the world actually works that way. Obviously, they face repeated disappointments as they see that life is not like their Little League experience: They don't get a trophy after every season.

We have also learned that people don't develop a healthy sense of self by being told how great they are. While it's certainly true that children need unconditional love and encouragement, trying to build their "self-concept" *for them* implies that a healthy sense of self is gained by being given things rather than earning them.

A healthy sense of self is largely developed from the *inside out* when parents provide the following:

- Unconditional love rather than constant praise, attention, or rewards.
- Opportunities to make choices and experience the consequences, both positive and negative.
- The gift of occasionally experiencing disappointments and struggles.
- Just enough guidance so that their children can see themselves overcoming these trials—but not so much that we parents are simply doing everything for them.
- Plenty of experiences where the kids see that they have what it takes to cope and solve problems if they work hard and persevere.

Let's consider little Benjamin and his daddy. Is Pop guiding his son toward a healthy sense of self?

"No!" Benjie's dad said. "That's not how you do it. You have to make the two loops and then cross them. Why aren't you listening?"

"Dumb laces! I hate tying my shoes. I can't do it!"

"Benjie," Dad answered sternly, "just let me do it. I don't know why you never listen. What am I going to do with you?"

❤ ❤ ❤

Every time Benjamin is treated this way constitutes a "withdrawal" from his healthy sense-of-self account. Despite the fact that his father is the last person to wish discouragement on his son, he is unwittingly helping to create it.

Let's imagine Benjie's dad has learned some Love and Logic:

"My car is leaving when the timer on the stove goes *ding*. Are you going to school with your shoes tied or the laces just tucked inside?"

Benjie is not happy. "Dumb laces! I can't do it! Tucking in makes it scratchy."

Dad answers empathetically, "I bet that does make it scratchy."

"But I can't do it!" Benjie whines.

"Would you like some ideas?" asks Dad.

"What?"

"Well, Benjie, some kids decide to cross the two loops like this. See if you can do it on this shoe. You can watch me as I do the other."

"It's hard!"

"I know. It was really hard for me when I was four."

"It was hard for you, too?" Benjie asks with eyes wide.

"Yes, it was—but you can do it. Watch me."

With fumbling fingers, little Benjamin loops the laces and manages a rather interesting knot. "I did it just like your one!" he shrieks with joy.

"You can do things when you keep trying. Give me five!" ◀))

❤ ❤ ❤

In this second scenario, Benjamin's daddy gave him a gift. He allowed Benjie to struggle a bit with the problem—instead of getting frustrated and simply solving it for him. With unconditional love and wise questions, he let Benjie make a decision, and learn that he was capable.

When did Benjie receive empathy instead of criticism? When did he begin to experience how it feels to succeed, to see himself as a thinking, competent, and strong little boy?

How Parents Determine a Child's Sense of Self

FORMULA FOR AN UNHEALTHY ONE...

Parents who:

- Find faults, criticize, and show anger and frustration.
- Insist on doing everything for their children.
- Don't allow their children to experience the joy of independent success.
- Try to make sure their kids always win and everything is easy and fun.
- Demonstrate love to their kids only when they behave.

FORMULA FOR A HEALTHY ONE...

Parents who:

- Offer empathy, understanding, and unconditional love.
- Allow their children to struggle and solve their own problems.
- Allow their children to lose games from time to time, so they learn how to persevere.
- Allow children to experience the gratification of seeing perseverance pays off.
- Demonstrate unconditional love.

The Gift of Effort-Related Success

A goal of Love and Logic is to make the home as similar as possible to the real world. Our children must know how to handle situations that appear without warning—that require them to think for themselves. When we give our children this gift, they begin to believe: "I've got what it takes!"

Take a look at Wyatt, a child who learned a lesson one day while playing with a friend. One person wanted to rescue him, another wanted to empower him to feel good about his ability to handle life. To rescue or not to rescue? That is the question.

Wyatt is playing at the park as his mom and grandmother sit nearby, sipping coffee and enjoying the peaceful day. All is right with the world—that is, until another preschooler joins him in the sandbox.

Wyatt suddenly runs to his mother, screaming and pointing at the boy, "Mommy! That kid is throwing sand! And he said that I still wear diapers!"

"Wow," Mom empathizes, "that's really upsetting. What do you think you are going to do?" ◀)

Both Wyatt and his grandmother are shocked. He answers, "You tell him to stop!"

Grandma agrees with her precious grandson. She turns to her daughter and urges, "Go tell that boy to stop being so mean."

Mom smiles at Wyatt and suggests, "Some kids decide to play on the slide or the swings instead of playing with a kid who is being mean. Some decide to tell him that they will play with him if he acts nice. I can't wait to see how you handle this."

Wyatt is thinking so hard that smoke is starting to pour from his ears. "Should I play someplace else or...?" he wonders.

Soon, he's off to the sandbox to see if he can make a friend. On the way home he chatters away, "I didn't think that kid—his name is James—was going to be nice. He was mean at first but then I told him that I only play with kids that are nice. He started being nice. Then we played on the swings. He said he was kidding about me wearing diapers. He has a cat and two dogs, and one of them has three legs. And then…"

❤ ❤ ❤

Wyatt was given a great gift—the gift of wisdom. Every time we ask questions and provide some suggestions, instead of merely rescuing, we give them tools that will last a lifetime. Mom saw the opportunity for Wyatt to learn something valuable. While she was certainly ready and willing to rescue if need be, she resisted the urge so her wonderful little boy could see that he's got what it takes to make it in life.

Weighing learning to cope with challenges versus being rescued from them, which will develop a healthy and strong sense of self?

Every time we rescue our children, we erode their confidence and ability to make good decisions. Each time they persevere and solve a problem, we help build them up.

PRINCIPLE #2: *Share Control within Limits*

Have you ever dropped coins into a vending machine—and nothing came out, including the coins? Have you ever misplaced your TV remote control or cell phone? Have you ever waited in line at the grocery store when the clerk closes up just as it's finally your turn? Has a video you were trying to watch online taken forever to load? Has your car ever failed to start when you were already late for an appointment?

Why are these situations so frustrating? They are irritating largely because the situation feels out of control. No matter how hard we kick the vending machine, nothing comes out. No matter how many times we turn the key, our car will not start. We feel powerless. It's that simple. Control is a basic human emotional need. It's something we crave so strongly that sometimes people will even hurt others—or themselves—to regain it. If you've ever seen a driver suddenly pull out from behind you, veer into another lane, and almost cause a head-on accident, you've seen the result of unmet control desires.

When children lack a sense of healthy control, some very sad things can happen.

Aubrey's parents were controlling with her while she was growing up. Her entire life was filled with rules. She was given no choices and was always told how to dress, how to walk, what to say, how to say it, how to complete all of her school assignments, and whom she should choose as friends.

"Don't do that!" her parents would say as she reached for colorful objects. "Don't cry!" they would say when she burst into tears. Her life was full of don'ts, and she never had opportunities to make decisions that concerned her welfare.

When she became a teenager, her parents simply said, "Don't do drugs, don't have sex, and don't meet people online." There were no discussions, no questions about how Aubrey felt about drugs, sex, or cyber dating. When her parents found out that she was pregnant, they were shocked.

"We told her time and time again to be careful about those things!" her father lamented. "The girl doesn't listen!" added her mother.

❤ ❤ ❤

Sadly, we at the Love and Logic Institute are not surprised. Aubrey had found a way to show her parents that she was the one in control. Never experiencing healthy control, she gravitated toward the unhealthy variety.

The Art and Science of Sharing Control within Limits

Battles over control benefit no one. They create tension and make warriors out of otherwise peaceful people. Love and Logic teaches parents the science of control. What is this "science"?

Share control when you don't need it, so you can get some back when you do.

Love and Logic also teaches the art of sharing control within limits. What is this "art"? Share control by giving the types of choices that never cause a problem for you. And very importantly, offer these choices before your child gets resistant—not afterward.

> Sammy's father asked him, "Do you think it would be a good day to have fun at the park, or do you think it would be a good day to not have fun at the park?"
>
> Sammy's eyes lit up, he got this funny look on his face, and he said, "Fun at the park, silly!"
>
> Dad is sharing control with some fun choices. Mom decides to join the fun.
>
> "Okay. Now, let's see," she adds. "Do you want me to put your car seat on the left side of the backseat, or the right side?"
>
> "I want to sit in the front!" says Sammy.
>
> "Oh, that wasn't a choice. Let's put you on the right side." Not giving his child a chance to complain, Sammy's dad moves forward quickly. "Do you want me to drive the speed limit, or do you want me to drive a bit slower?"
>
> "I want you to drive the speed limit, so we can get there fast!" Sammy says, partly exasperated by all these questions, but at the same time, feeling a great sense of control in telling his father how to drive the car—within limits.
>
> When they get to the park, Sammy's mother asks, "Do you want to get on the swing first, or would you rather get on the slide?"
>
> "I want to swing first!"
>
> "Okay," says his dad. "Do you want me to push you, or do you want to swing by yourself?"
>
> "Push me!" Sammy says, all excited.
>
> "You want me to push you hard, or soft?"

"Hard!"

"Oh, okay," says his father. "Do you want to fall off and hurt yourself, or not fall off and hurt yourself?"

"Not!" says Sammy, perfectly seriously.

"Okay," says Sammy's mother. "You said you wanted to go on the slide. Do you want me to go on with you, or do you want me to stay here and watch?"

"You watch!" he says.

"You want me to catch you like a big monster and scare you when you come down, or do you want me to stand here and just be quiet?"

The wonderful thing about sharing this kind of control with young kids is that we can get silly with it and make it fun for ourselves as well as our kids.

Sammy's mother notices that they have another fifteen minutes until they need to go. She signals her husband.

Sammy's dad asks, "Sammy, would you like to leave now, or would you like to leave in fifteen minutes?"

"Fifteen minutes," Sammy says, happily claiming his control as if he's just won a prize.

When the time expires, Dad says, "Okay! Fifteen minutes is over. Let's go."

Sammy immediately responds, "I don't want to go!"

Mom smiles and whispers, "Now, didn't we give you a lot of choices? This time it's our turn for a choice. Thanks for understanding."

With that information, Sammy looks at the dirt and whispers reluctantly, "Well—okay."

❤ ❤ ❤

Sammy's parents shared gobs of control by providing plenty of choices. Did you notice that these choices were framed by firm limits? Did you notice how they were careful to give choices only on issues that did not create a problem for anyone on the planet? Did you notice how they provided choices before he became resistant—not after?

When we provide choices before a child becomes resistant, we share healthy control.

When we provide choices after they complain or resist, we reward them for complaining and resisting.

Did you also see how Sammy responded to this approach? Are you guessing that your children are going to be far happier and better prepared for life if they experience the same? Are you guessing your entire family will experience more joy as they grow?

Remember that choices are only one-half of the picture. The other involves providing and enforcing loving limits.

Some parents set too few limits with their toddlers.

Then they attempt to regain control of their home when their kids become teens.

By that time, it might be too late.

Love and Logic parents avoid the pain caused by waiting to set limits until their children are teens. Why? Because they understand that a child's ability to make choices, within the safety of limits, is the foundation of responsibility and wisdom—and they want to lay that foundation as early as possible. These parents also understand that even though children outwardly throw tantrums or complain about limits, inwardly they yearn for their parents to set and enforce them.

Sharing control within firm limits teaches wisdom and responsibility. Let's take a look at how one parent used a masterful combination of choices and limits to begin teaching responsibility.

Jim gazed lovingly at his little Cindy and asked, "Sweetie? Will you be picking up your toys today, or will I?"

When she forgot, he quietly picked them up and placed them on the top shelf of the hallway closet. Love and Logic parents know children learn best from consequences when their parents avoid reminding or scolding. Jim kept his mouth shut and kept saying to himself, "Let the consequence do the teaching. Let the consequence do the teaching. Let the consequence do the teaching."

The next day, Cindy was a bit confused. "Where are my toys, Daddy?" she asked.

Jim responded softly, "How sad. Remember yesterday when I gave you a choice—to either pick them up or have me do it?"

"Yes, Daddy," she replied.

"Guess what happened?"

"You put them up?" she whined.

Jim simply nodded and whispered, "Yes, this is so sad. What can you do to earn them back?"

Cindy cried out, "But I want my toys! I want to play with them today!"

Jim continued, "You may have them when you've helped with some things like dusting or picking up the yard. I will have some time to help tomorrow after work. Are you going to stop yelling, or do you need to have some 'being quiet' practice time in your room?" 🔊

Cindy stopped yelling and started to weep softly. Jim looked at her and asked, "Would you like a hug or no hug?"

Cindy looked up and said softly, "Hug."

The next evening Cindy helped her daddy dust the baseboards, pick up the yard, and take out the trash. The next morning he gladly returned her toys, secretly hoping she'd have another Love and Logic training session. Cindy began playing with them but was quickly distracted by something else. Jim walked by and asked, "Cindy, will you be cleaning up your toys today, or will you be letting me?"

Cindy ran over and began tossing them into her toy chest. Jim couldn't resist asking, "Why are you picking them up instead of letting me?"

"Silly Daddy!" she responded. "I'm going to play with them tomorrow!"

❤ ❤ ❤

PRINCIPLE #3: *Provide a Strong Dose of Empathy Before Delivering Consequences*

There are many psychological theories about the role that discomfort plays in learning. Most suggest that human beings are programmed to avoid it. This makes sense. Most sane people will touch a hot stove only once before learning not to make a career out of it. As you may have learned from personal experience, when we hurt, we are often moved to make changes we might not otherwise make.

Similarly, Love and Logic parents know that the pain of poor choices helps children learn to avoid mistakes. They also know that for this to happen, the child must not be able to blame their pain on the parent's anger:

Consequences provided with anger = resentment and rebellion

Consequences provided with empathy = learning and self-control

Let's be clear. Love and Logic parents don't use consequences to punish their kids into behaving. They use them to guide their children toward learning how to make themselves behave.

Punishment is about making kids "pay" for their bad behavior. Love and Logic consequences are all about helping our children learn from it—so they can lead self-controlled, happy lives.

Learning to Avoid Life-and-Death Mistakes

Love and Logic parents love it when their children make small, affordable mistakes. Why? Because the price tags of mistakes made by young children are much smaller than those made by teens. What's the price tag of wasting one's allowance at age five? It's insignificant. What's the price tag of wasting one's paycheck at age twenty-one? That's another story. What's the price tag of crashing one's tricycle? Perhaps a skinned knee. What's the price tag of crashing one's car at age sixteen? Perhaps one's life.

At the Love and Logic Institute, we believe children pay dearly when not allowed to make mistakes—and learn from them—when consequences are still small and "affordable."

Robert's dad, Steve, had not gone fishing in a long time, and he was looking forward to this trip. This time Steve was taking his son, who was going fishing for the first time. They were both excited; however, by the time they made the hour-long drive, little Robert was what we call "three-quarters cranky"—not really a problem yet, but getting there.

Robert started to whine, "I don't want to go fishing. This is boring. It's cold up here."

"Well," said Steve, "let's give it a try since we came all this way." The two of them found a shallow part of the lake and walked out to where it was only about a foot deep. There were some mossy rocks—fairly flat and not very high—jutting out of the water.

When Steve looked up, he saw Robert starting to climb one of the low rocks. He thought to himself, "I better warn him and tell him to get off that rock. He's going to fall in. I know he is."

What does a wise Love and Logic parent do at this point? The first question is always, "Will my child get hurt if he makes a mistake?"

Steve quickly reviewed the situation. "It's sandy here, not high, but he could get cold." The second question a parent asks is, "What will the child learn from this?" Steve thought, "He'll never do it again!"

A second later, Steve heard a big splash. He turned and saw Robert jumping out of the water moving toward his father. "Daddy," Robert cried, "you didn't tell me that rocks get slippery when they're wet!"

"Well," asked his father, with warmth and sadness in his voice, "what do you think?"

"I think they do!" little Robert said, as his dad pulled a towel from his backpack and wrapped it around his son.

"You're right!" said Steve. "You figured that out."

❤ ❤ ❤

Do you think Steve contributed to Robert developing a healthy sense of self by letting him make the slippery rock discovery on his own? Yes, because Robert could see himself learning something. Did Steve enjoy watching his son fall in? No, but he allowed it. He let it happen because he knew it would be a safe, yet powerful learning opportunity. The next time they went fishing, do you think little Robert watched the rocks closely to be sure of his footing? Absolutely. Robert is older now and loves to go fishing with his dad. From time to time, he even reminds his dad to be more careful.

How do Love and Logic parents look upon their young children's mistakes? With great joy! Rather than getting angry or frustrated, they see mistakes as opportunities for their kids to think. They ask questions, wait for answers, and make heavy deposits into their children's wisdom accounts.

Unfortunately, some parents short-circuit or destroy the learning value of mistakes. How? By lecturing or responding with sternness or anger. Would Robert have learned so quickly about slippery rocks if Dad had responded with, "See! That's what you get! I hope you learned your lesson!"?

Why Anger Short-Circuits Learning

The "fight or flight" response exists in all human beings and is part of the "primitive" brain—that part of the brain governing basic survival instincts. When we feel threatened or in danger, our brain tells us, "This is unsafe! Get ready to fight, or get ready to run away!" When we deliver consequences with anger, children's brains go into "survival" mode rather than "learning" mode. They think more about escaping, or possibly getting revenge, than about how to make smarter choices in the future. In the survival mode, we cannot learn. Our focus is on getting away, fighting to be free, surviving.

**Every time we use empathy, our kids'
reasoning brains turn on.**

**Every time we deliver threats or anger, their reasoning brains
turn off. Empathy opens the mind to learning.**

When parents provide empathy before delivering consequences, there is no "fight or flight" response. Caught in the flood of heartfelt understanding from a parent, a child is much less likely to become too angry or scared to learn. Under these circumstances, a child is also less likely to blame others for his or her mistake. Kids who are given empathy quickly develop a healthy voice inside of their heads. Instead of blaming or shifting responsibility, this voice asks, "How is my next decision going to affect my life? Which choice is going to be the wisest?" When our children face consequences, our spoonful of empathy is what makes the medicine of learning go down. Rather than set ourselves up as the enemy, wise parents use empathy in a way that makes the child's mistake the "bad guy," while keeping them, the parents, the "good guys." ◄»

Anger vs. Sincere Empathy

Consequences with Anger

Parent is stern or acts with anger:

- "Stop spitting that food! Quit it! That's it! I'm sick and tired of this! You'll just have to go hungry!"
- "For crying out loud! If you would just take care of your toys, they wouldn't break. No! I won't buy you another. What do you think? Do you think money grows on trees?"
- "No, I am not taking you out for pizza. What do you expect after the way you behaved last time? I hope this teaches you a lesson!"
- "Quit that whining! How many times do I have to tell you? Stop it! Go to your room!"

Consequences with Sincere Empathy

Parent says softly:

- "How sad. Dinner is over."
- "Bummer. I feel so sad when I break my things."
- "This is so sad. We can have pizza sometime when I don't have to worry about tantrums at the restaurant."
- "Uh-oh. Looks like a little bedroom time."

Remember:
Sincere empathy works wonders.
Sarcastic empathy backfires every time.

PRINCIPLE #4: *Share the Thinking*

Aria, a sixteen-year-old high school student, is driving some friends home from volleyball practice. As she pulls into heavy traffic, she hears her phone buzz. Someone has just sent her a text.

From the backseat, one of the girls yells, "Like aren't you going to get that? Like it's probably Riley."

Another chimes in, "What's wrong with you? It's probably about the party on Saturday. Get it!"

Is Aria now in the position of having to make a major life-and-death decision? ◄»

❤ ❤ ❤

Children and teens of all ages encounter massive peer pressure and temptation nearly every day of their lives. What largely determines whether they will resist texting while driving, doing drugs, visiting inappropriate websites, shoplifting, having sex, etc.? The factors that determine whether Aria will resist or succumb largely took place during the first five or six years of her life. Let's ask ourselves some questions.

- **How is Aria's Sense of Self?** How does Aria see herself? Does she feel capable of making good decisions and enjoying the positive consequences of these decisions, or does she lack healthy confidence and can only feel good about herself if she is pleasing all of her peers?

- **Does Aria have a healthy sense of personal control?** Has she been allowed to share control with her parents, or has she been prevented from having any? Is there any chance Aria might immediately reply to Riley's text because she needs so badly to exert some independence or to show her parents who's really in control?

- **Does Aria have a strong relationship with her parents?** Does she enjoy pleasing them because she looks up to them? Or would nothing make her happier than to upset them?

- **Has she made plenty of mistakes and learned from them at an early age?** Has Aria already made lots of mistakes, experienced lots of empathy, and been held accountable? Does she have a healthy voice inside her head asking, "How is this next decision going to affect my life?"?

- **Has Aria had lots of practice making choices, solving problems, and thinking for herself?** Has she had the opportunity to make decisions, think about her blunders, and consider their consequences? Or has someone else always told her what to do, solved her problems, and stolen any opportunity for her to practice thinking for herself?

Four Powerful Actions

There are four powerful actions parents can take to raise kids who wind up making smart decisions about technology, drugs, alcohol, sex, and other serious matters. It's never too early to...

1. Raise a child with a healthy and strong sense of self.
2. Develop a strong bond of love and trust with your child.
3. Allow your child to make plenty of mistakes and learn from them at an early age.
4. Give your child plenty of practice thinking and solving problems.

All four of these powerful gifts allow children to develop stronger thinking skills.

How do we prepare our children for the tough, sometimes life-and-death decisions they'll have to make? The first step is showing that we care.

Every time we replace anger with empathy and caring, we help a child become better prepared to make wise decisions.

The more empathy and understanding we display, the more our children are forced to think about the pain they have created for themselves. The more anger or frustration we show, the less our children think—and the less they learn about solving problems.

Shared thinking means applying massive doses of love and empathy. It means guiding children toward solutions rather than either rescuing or automatically doling out punishment. It all starts when we ask thoughtful questions.

"What a bummer, Ricky," the mother says to her five-year-old. "You gave your little sister a haircut, and now one side is really long, and the other is short and crooked. What are you going to do?"

Ricky scrunches up his shoulders and mumbles, "Don't know."

Mom responds softly, "Would you like to hear some ideas?"

"Uh-huh."

"One idea is to open your piggy bank and find enough money to have one of the ladies at Awesome Clips fix it. How will that work?"

Ricky's eyes light up. "That sounds good, Mommy. How much will it cost?"

"I'm not sure. I'll show you how to call them, and you can ask how much they charge."

Ricky's little fingers push the buttons, he utters his question, listens, says goodbye, and hangs up. Tears are now running down his cheeks. Sniffling, he says, "She said it's gonna cost more dollars than I have! What I s'posed to do?"

Mom replies with empathy, "This is so sad." She pauses to add a little drama. "Want another idea?"

Ricky nods his head "yes."

"You can earn the other money by helping me with a bunch of chores around here, like dusting and pulling up weeds in the yard. How would that work?"

Ricky looks up and says, "I hate chores."

Mom responds, "Another idea is to pay me with your Cyber Stanley Action Figure. How would that..."

With half-dollar-sized eyes, Ricky interrupts, "I'll do chores. I'll do chores!"

❤ ❤ ❤

Did you notice how much thinking Ricky had to do? Does Ricky get better prepared for the real world every time he has to make some difficult decisions and choices? And does Ricky's mom have a lot more fun now that she's handling the problem with Love and Logic?

The principles of Love and Logic were developed when we were searching for common threads that might help us look at human behavior in a new way. Here's what we discovered.

Successful people never fail, because they turn their failures into wisdom.

THE FOUR PRINCIPLES OF LOVE AND LOGIC

1. **Help Children Build a Healthy Sense of Self.** Everything kids learn and do affects how they see themselves. This in turn, determines what they choose to do with their lives.

2. **Share Control Within Limits.** Control is like love. The more we give away, the more we get in return. When we love people, we will also set healthy limits.

3. **Offer Empathy, Then Consequences.** Empathy allows children to learn from their mistakes instead of learning to resent adults.

4. **Share the Thinking.** Give your kids a lifelong gift. Every time they cause a problem or make a mistake, allow them to think more about the solution than you do.

The Result: Loving Relationships

Each of these principles builds strong, self-controlled, and responsible kids. Each also contributes to lifelong loving relationships. Always remember:

**Limits, consequences—and all other
parenting techniques—will fail miserably without
loving relationships.**

In other words, successful people keep learning, and they never give up. When we learned how well this applies to adults, we thought, how about kids?

We believe, from watching the young children in our own lives, as well as those we've met in our many years of work and travel, that it's never too early to start teaching wisdom.

Wouldn't it be great if your children could learn, early on, that every choice they make affects the quality of their lives? A combination of love and logic can create this learning now, while they are still very young.

**Love allows children to grow
through their mistakes.**

**Logic happens when we allow them to live with
the consequences of their choices.**

Love and Logic Experiment #1

Sharing Control Within Limits

Make a list of possible choices you can give your kids.

Here are some examples:
- "Would you like milk or juice with breakfast?"
- "Are you going to put your shirt on first or your pants on first?"
- "Are you going to wear your red shorts or your blue ones?"
- "Are you going to wear your coat or just carry it?"
- "Do you want a story before bed or no story?"
- "Do you want your night-light on or off?"
- "Are you going to brush your teeth now or in five minutes?"
- "Are you going to have carrots or peas for your vegetable?"

Remember to follow the Love and Logic guidelines for choices.

- Give 99 percent of choices when things are going smoothly.
- Provide choices before your child gets resistant—not after.
- Provide choices only on issues that are not dangerous and don't create a problem for anyone else on the planet.
- Always offer two options, each a choice that makes you happy.
- Within five to ten seconds, choose for the child if he or she hasn't made a choice.

See how many "deposits" you can make during the day.

See how many choices you can give during the day. Every choice you give becomes a "deposit" into your child's sense of healthy control. Have some fun. Even when choices seem small and a bit silly, they can be powerful.

Make a healthy "withdrawal" and see how your child reacts.

Pick an issue and choose not to give your child a choice. For example, "Please go to bed. Thank you."

If your child says something like, "I don't want to," try saying, "Don't I give you lots of choices? This time it's my turn. Thank you." In Love and Logic language, we call this a healthy "withdrawal." The more healthy deposits of control we provide, the more likely we'll gain cooperation when we have to make a healthy withdrawal by simply telling them what to do.

See how your child reacts. Parents tell us over and over that the more choices, or "deposits" they make, the more cooperative their kids become when they need to make a healthy withdrawal.

CHAPTER TWO

It's Never Too Early to Start

Better Now Than Later

Over the last four decades, people have shared many fun Love and Logic success stories. Some have even used it successfully on their spouses! Kids can be a challenge, but with a few Love and Logic tools, you can up the odds that the early years—and beyond—will be a joy. What's the most important advice we give parents? Start as early in your child's life as possible.

Imagine that you've joined a camping trip for parents and their toddlers, and you're out in the wild, sharing this joyful experience with your four-year-old, who's been enjoying the new scenery, the crunchy, colored leaves, the tiny creatures he's discovered on the ground, and the sounds of the forest.

On the trip is a mother with a strong-willed toddler. Suddenly, the peacefulness of the forest is pierced by her child's whiney demands. "Mommy, look! Mommy, come! Mommy, stop! I'm tired! Whaaaa! Mommy, I don't like! Mommy, Mommy, Mommy!"

The mother looks at you with some embarrassment and says, laughing nervously, "Jake is always so bossy. I don't know why."

You smile politely and move on, but you think to yourself, "I know why." This is a mother who is allowing her little boy to treat her like a doormat. This mom is waiting until "later" to teach her child about responsibility and treating others with respect. You hope that she doesn't wait too much longer. ◄))

❤ ❤ ❤

Why do some parents wait too long to begin setting and enforcing limits? Why do some allow their toddlers to get out of control and begin running the home? Some parents believe that young children are too young to learn. Don't fall into this trap!

Four Common Myths about Discipline

Let's take a look at four common myths about discipline and young children.

MYTH #1: *Discipline and Learning Require Language*

Some people believe children cannot learn or benefit from positive discipline until they can converse. Nothing is further from the truth. Can the family dog learn how to sit, stay, come, fetch, and lie down? I've never met a pooch who talked, but I have met some parents who seemed to believe and act like the family dog is smarter than their kids. How sad!

By the age of nine months, children are more intelligent than any creature on the planet. Therefore, wise parents begin Love and Logic during the early months. They do so through simple, loving actions—not words. If their child, for example, throws her bottle, they remove it for a while. If their child won't sit in the highchair, they fasten his seatbelt. If their child runs away from them in the store, they pick him up and gently belt him into the stroller. They replace anger, lectures, threats, and repeated warnings with loving yet firm actions.

MYTH #2: *A Little Child Cannot Remember and Learn*

Have you ever promised a two-year-old a trip to the park or his favorite fast-food restaurant—and then forgotten to deliver? Will they ever let you forget? Never underestimate what young children can remember and learn.

MYTH #3: *Setting Limits Will Break a Young Child's Spirit*

Some parents worry about making their toddlers angry. These parents seem to reason, "If I make sure that she's happy all the time, then she'll grow up to be a happy, nice person."

Wrong! At the Love and Logic Institute we're all for happy kids. That's why we encourage parents to set limits early. Why? Children who are made happy all of the time by their parents, experience a major shock when they begin to grow up. Ironically, they soon become the most unhappy and demanding kids and adults you'll ever meet.

MYTH #4: *Limits and Consequences Interfere with Attachment*

As we've mentioned earlier—and will again throughout this book, we believe healthy bonding and attachment is essential. Wonderful books have been written on the subject. Some very misleading ones have also been published.

The misleading ones claim parents should never use limits or consequences, because doing so will upset children and make it impossible for them to remain bonded with their parents.

We agree that rules and punishments provided with anger, lectures, or sarcasm can be damaging to relationships. However, limits and consequences provided with sincere empathy actually build relationships and strengthen bonding. Children are more likely to develop strong attachment relationships with adults who are strong enough to calmly set and enforce limits. Why would anyone want to bond with a doormat?

The First Weeks of Life

Would you be surprised to discover that the ability to learn basic cause and effect begins during a child's first weeks of life? Here are a few things a child learns very, very early:

- Crying brings Mommy or Daddy!
- I can move my foot!
- When I smile, Mommy and Daddy smile back!

> **A child's ability to learn**
> **basic cause and effect begins during**
> **the first weeks of life.**

During the first weeks and months of life, infants quickly figure out whether their parents are going to set limits or become doormats. Remember Jake, the whiney and demanding kid from the camping trip? Are you guessing that he received plenty of healthy limits when he was smaller—or way too few?

Love and Logic is all about being a good model for your kids by taking care of yourself in loving ways. Here's how Carter's mother accomplished this.

I (Jim) was sitting in a restaurant booth behind Carter and his mom. He looked to be just under two, and I knew he was normal when he began to whine about his lunch. His loving mother was very slow to respond.

"Mommy," Carter said, "why you not listening?"

His mother softly replied, "Carter, honey, why do you think?"

"But why?" he continued.

Pausing briefly from her meal, she sweetly repeated her question, "Why do you think?"

Carter became silent for a few seconds, then sweetened the tone of his voice and said, "You listen big boy words?"

"Oh, yes," she said warmly. "You figured that out all by yourself!"

Still in a sweet tone of voice, he asked, "I don't eat?"

Mom answered, "You decide how much you eat. I'm eating because dinner is a long time from now."

Carter perked up. "All I get?"

Mom answered, "What do you think?"

He replied, "I be starving to deaf!"

Mom giggled. "Yeah. You might be hungry if you don't eat enough before dinner, but, Carter, I will still love you. You get to decide. Give me a hug."

While Carter only ate about a third of his sandwich and fruit, does it appear that he's learning some healthy lessons about how to talk to his mommy? Is he also learning about how much food his tummy needs?

❤ ❤ ❤

Which kid would you rather be around? Jake or Carter? Which child do you think will lead a happier life in the long run?

**When people ask, "When can we start using
Love and Logic with our children?" we say,
"Start when they're babies.
Start when they're cute, so they will stay that way!"**

Bonding Builds Trust and Responsibility

When our children are infants, our primary goal must be to develop a strong, caring bond of attachment. Why is this bond so essential? In the following chapter, we'll learn that bonding builds a foundation of trust that lasts a lifetime. Furthermore, this foundation of trust influences every relationship a person ever experiences.

Children without this foundation tend to experience chronic relationship problems and severe anger, and often become destructive to themselves and others.

How is this foundation constructed? Every time our infant cries, and we respond by meeting his or her needs, we put in place another building block of trust. On a deep emotional level, the child reasons, "The world is a good place—and I'm good!"

Bonding Requires Limit-Setting

In the next chapter, we'll also learn that bonding requires basic limit-setting. When children fail to find loving limits, they feel scared. How do they tell us? By acting out.

> **When children act out,
> what they're really saying is,
> "Please love me enough to set some limits!"**

Little ten-month-old Linda was beginning to resist the strained carrots her mother, Selena, was offering her for lunch. At first, Linda had seemed to enjoy the carrots. Then, little by little, she became crankier and crankier. Suddenly she became so cranky that she spit them out— all over the tray, her highchair, her bib—and her mommy.

Selena immediately put down Linda's tiny spoon and said, with gentle, sweet sorrow in her voice, "How sad. Lunch is over." She quickly but gently raised the tray of her daughter's highchair, lifted Linda out of her seat, and took her to her crib. She said nothing more.

❤ ❤ ❤

Did you notice how Mom used Love and Logic to lock in the empathy? Did you notice how Mom used simple, loving actions instead of anger, lectures, or threats? This child may be very young, but she's already learning about limits, consequences, and how much her mommy loves her.

The "Terrible Twos" Can Be Terrific

We often hear people argue that two-year-olds are too young to benefit from Love and Logic, because they can't understand or remember. At the Love and Logic Institute, we don't agree, and here's why. Have you ever promised a two-year-old a lollipop and failed to deliver? Have you ever told your toddler you would take him to his favorite ice cream shop and then forgotten to make the trip? If so, you'll have to acknowledge what we've learned at Love and Logic: By age two, long-term memory is firmly locked in.

Meet Curtis. Like many kids his age, Curtis's favorite word is "no." He loves the sound of the word and says it many times in the course of a day. While his mother used to interpret this as Curtis's way of being disagreeable and ornery, she's learned that it's really a natural behavior for a two-year-old. Best of all, she now has some skills for handling it.

> The primary developmental task of a toddler is to establish autonomy, and Curtis loves to practice being autonomous! "No!" he says when his mother asks him to hold her hand. "No!" he shouts when she asks him to wait for her. "No!" he yells when she tells him not to leave an aisle without her.
>
> When they went shopping, Curtis loved to run away from his mother in the store. As much as his mother understood his desire for independence, his brief disappearances would make her nervous. She decided to take some action.
>
> Unbeknownst to Curtis, she had a friend follow her to the store and wait in the parking lot. As Mom began her shopping, Curtis wandered. This was a dream come

true for Curtis's mom. He was misbehaving, and this was her opportunity to give Curtis a gift of wisdom.

As she caught up with him, she dialed her cell phone and said, "Okay, it's time. Come and get him."

Curtis's eyes grew to the size of coffee can lids as Mom's friend led him out of the store. He was even unhappier when he had to use his Zooming Wheels Racer to pay for the baby-sitting. What a bummer.

The following week, Curtis's mom was getting ready to go shopping. She said to Curtis, "I have to go shopping, sweetie. Do you want to come with me?"

"Yes!" announced Curtis, using a word he rarely uses.

"What's the rule when we go shopping, honey?"

"I stay with Mommy!" Curtis responded, without missing a beat.

"That's right," his mother said. "Way to go!"

When they reached the store, Curtis was so excited that he experienced temporary memory impairment. What did Mom do? With a lilt in her voice, she sang, "Uh-oh!"

Curtis quickly looked up at his mother, smiled, and ran to her side. From that day on, shopping became a pleasure instead of a pain—for both of them.

❤ ❤ ❤

Curtis's mommy conducted a Love and Logic training session. Did you notice how she replaced anger with empathy? Did you notice how Curtis got a chance to learn about limits, consequences, and cause and effect? Did Curtis have to do some thinking on his own, or did his mother rescue him? Do you suppose Curtis sees his mom as strong and loving at the same time?

When It's Time for Potty Training

There are many wonderful ways to help our kids think for themselves and help them become wiser. The following is a story about Harry, who learned, along with his family, that potty training can be fun, for both parent and child.

Little Harry lives in a house that has two bathrooms—one upstairs and one downstairs. One morning, his father said, "Hey, Harry! You want to use the upstairs potty or the downstairs potty?"

"Upstairs! Upstairs potty!" Harry said.

A Love and Logic parent, his father smiled and said, "You want to have fun while we're doing this, or not have fun?"

The great thing about choices with little kids is that they love making them—even when the options we give seem a bit silly to us. The decisions they make on their own make them feel important, leave them with a sense of control, and give them lots of chances to exercise their brains.

Harry looked at his dad as if he were crazy and giggled, "Fun! I want to have fun!"

"Great," said his dad. "Do you want to bring a drink in with you, or do you want to wait until you're done?"

"Wait till I'm done!"

"Do you want to bring Clarence, your stuffed sea otter, with us, or do you want to leave him?"

"Bring him!" Harry says, as he goes to retrieve his favorite stuffed playmate.

Now, Harry's dad moves to the next step—modeling. Although some parents might find it a little embarrassing, modeling is the best way to teach your kids just about anything. Harry's dad thinks it's great.

"Hey! I really have to use the bathroom!" he says enthusiastically to his son. "Why don't you come in with me? Let's go. Let me show you how it's done!"

He shows his son how he uses the bathroom. "This is so much fun!" he laughs. "Someday when you're big enough, I bet you'll be able to use the potty like me.

Then you can have fun, too. Boy, I love using the potty!
I can even wipe myself. Check this out!" He flushes the
toilet and waves, "Bye-bye!" as they look into the toilet.

❤ ❤ ❤

The logic here is clear. Kids want to be like their parents.
Whatever parents do, kids naturally want to be able to do, too.
And if parents think it's fun, kids will, too. So, parents have
some choices when it comes to potty training:

- We can allow ourselves to become embarrassed and refuse
  to model this skill.
- We can succumb to pressure from our friends, family,
  and society and try to potty train our kids before they
  are ready.
- We can fight endless power struggles by trying to force
  the issue.
- We can get angry and frustrated when they have accidents
  or regress.
- Or—we can choose to have some fun, take our time,
  build strong relationships with our kids and keep the
  process natural. How?
    + Model, model, and model some more.
    + Provide plenty of choices within limits.
    + Be silly.

**When parents model, offer choices, and make a task fun,
learning happens quickly.**

When Accidents Happen

If you know how to ride a bike, you probably remember
falling a few times before finding the right balance. When we're
learning something new, accidents are bound to happen. So it is
with our children when they are at potty-training age.

Successful parents dole out empathy and say, "Oh, you had an accident! That's too bad! I love you, sweetie." They take their time and don't rush anything, because there's no set timetable for potty training. Every child has his or her own unique schedule of development. ◀)

Some children potty train at two, some when they're four, and some at every age in between. It all depends on the child. A wise parent locks in the empathy and waits for kids to develop the skill on their own. Then, when a child is successful, a parent can say, "You did it! I bet that feels great!"

Unsuccessful parents have a pattern, too. When their kids make a mistake, they get upset or angry. They say, "You messed your pants again! That's not nice! We don't do that! Now you better learn how to do this right! You're going to sit here until you use the potty!"

You can guess what happens. The child sees frustrated parents, and the child gets frustrated, too. The more we understand how the brain learns, the more we see that effective learning cannot take place under conditions of anxiety or stress, particularly when the task is a rather difficult one.

I (Charles) often equate potty training with learning how to golf. Imagine that you are fairly new to the sport, and you've decided to get some lessons. As you are preparing for your swing, the coach, criticizes, "No! That's not right. You need to stand—no, no, not like that—aw, that's completely wrong. You aren't even listening to me!"

You finally manage to swing, driving the ball straight through the window of a nearby high-priced condo. Your coach throws up his arms, and says, "What were you thinking? I told you to point your toes this way. That's going to be expensive. But—that's what you get when you don't listen!"

Under such circumstances, would your brain be relaxed enough to learn, or would it be so stressed that all you could think about was either fighting back or fleeing? What are the chances that you'd feel exceptionally bonded with your coach and want to spend more time with him? What are the odds that you'll take up some other pastime instead?

Potty training—like reading, riding a bike, hitting a baseball, etc., is a complex skill, requiring mind-boggling levels of coordination among neurons and muscles. We often take this skill for granted and then assume that children who are having problems with it are simply being disobedient. Most of the time, this is not the case. Most of the time they are simply not quite ready.

Some Thoughts on Regression

The performance of any skill requiring developmental readiness rarely progresses in a steady path upward. Children don't learn and grow in the following fashion:

Not the way development really goes.

More accurately, the performance of acquiring developmental readiness proceeds in spurts, regressions, plateaus, spurts, plateaus, regressions—and so on:

The way that development really happens! ◀))

As a parent, have you ever felt like you were on a roller-coaster ride with your kids? A big part of this has to do with the normal process of development, where they seem to learn skills quickly, experience some dips, and even regress from time to time. As long as the "graph" is moving upward overall, there is no cause for panic.

Many parents express concern because their young child was using the potty and has stopped. Most of the time, this is normal and will resolve itself if the parents continue to remain relaxed. While the child may need to resume the use of diapers or pull-ups, this should be done without any anger, frustration, or shaming: "Sweetie, that's okay. Everybody makes mistakes."

Three Years and Beyond: Too Much Fun?

A parent, who'd been using Love and Logic with his three-year-old son, once asked, "Is it okay to be having this much fun? I've heard my friends complain about their kids, and frankly, I'm having a great time with mine. Am I doing something wrong?"

One of the beauties of Love and Logic is that it can make parenting fun again. When children reach the age of three, parents get to be even more creative. What makes this age so exciting? Kids are now able to do a lot more of their own thinking—and learning.

Oscar, the parent who had owned up to having so much fun, told us about his friend's child. Every morning, the mother has a fifteen-minute battle with her child over whether or not he is going to wear his coat. Oscar was bewildered. He kept remarking, "Why is the coat issue such a big deal? I never fight with my kid over that!"

To understand the difference between this child and Oscar's child, Natalie, we asked Oscar what he does. Here's his story.

Oscar said to his five-year-old daughter, Natalie, "Time to head for school. It's chilly out. Do you want to wear your coat, or do you want to carry it and see how long you can go without it?"

As soon as we heard Oscar's question, we immediately understood why he has no problem with Natalie. He gives her a choice, but both options mean she has to take her coat with her.

"I'll take it," Natalie said, "and see how long I can go without it."

As they drove to school, Natalie sat in the backseat and said, "I'm cold, Daddy. Turn up the heat." Natalie's coat was on the seat next to her.

Oscar described what he felt like saying: "Well, put your coat on!" Instead, he remembered his Love and Logic training and opted to say something a bit more loving and effective: "What do you think you can do?" Then he shut his mouth and waited a few seconds.

"Oh!" said Natalie, stopping to think and then declaring, "I better put on my coat."

❤ ❤ ❤

What did Natalie's father feel like saying in that moment? Again, probably something a bit sarcastic! But—again—he didn't. Instead, he said, "Good thinking! You figured that out by yourself! How did you do that?"

Natalie smiled, and said, "I made a good choice!"

Dad replied, "I bet that feels good." ◀》

Did you notice how her father held back the impulse to tell her what to do—or to put her down? Did you see how he did not rescue her, but allowed her to learn from her choice? Who was doing the thinking? Did you notice how her father's questions caused her to think and reach a decision on her own?

At the age of three and beyond, when kids are able to do more thinking for themselves, parents have many more opportunities to help build their healthy sense of self. Asking questions and allowing children to make decisions gives them skills they will use throughout their lives. It's never too early to start!

Children who can solve their own problems wind up feeling better about themselves.

So many kids! So little time! But because we're sure that these examples are helpful to parents, we want to offer you as many as we can. Over and over again, parents tell us how helpful these stories are to them. Here's a fun one about Lucas, who unwittingly grew a lot wiser one night after visiting with a relative.

Five-year-old Lucas spent the night with his cousin, Jayden. He had a great time. In fact, the two of them may have had too good of a time. The next day, as he dragged through the grocery store with his mother, she asked, "Why are you so tired?"

"'Cause me and Jayden stayed up all night watching videos and playing video games," Lucas whined.

Needless to say, Mom was irate—with Jayden's parents. Resisting the urge to vent, she replied, "Oh, that must have been fun." Now she had some time to calm down and reflect.

That evening, Mom complained to her husband, "I'm so mad! I can't believe they let the kids play video games all night. He's never going over there again."

As she vented, and as she calmed down, she began to remember Love and Logic: Wise parents hope and pray for mistakes when the price tags are small.

A couple of weeks later, Lucas was invited to another sleepover. His parents were ready to see how much their son had learned. As they neared Jayden's home, they asked playfully, "Hey, Lucas, are you going to stay up all night again? I think you should. Stay up all night, sweetie! Then when you come home, you can tell us all about it!"

"Yeah!" Lucas said excitedly. "That was so much fun last time!"

As you can imagine, Mom and Dad had a difficult time biting their tongues.

The next day, Lucas came home, and they couldn't wait to ask, "Did you make it all night? How many video games did you play?"

Lucas quickly answered, "I didn't want to play video games."

They inquired, "Why not? You said that it was so much fun."

"Yeah," he said, "but the last time I was so tired the next day!"

❤ ❤ ❤

While still angry with their kind, yet somewhat responsibility-challenged relatives, they realized they could not protect Lucas from "bad influences" for the rest of his life. "Maybe," they wondered, "it's better if he learns to deal with temptation and peer pressure now—under safe circumstances—rather than later under very dangerous ones.

Videos, Video Games, and other Screen Time: Use Caution!

As we saw above, Jayden's parents failed to understand something critically important: Children need limits. This also includes limits over how much time they spend staring at screens.

Since completing the first edition of this book, we've become increasingly concerned about the negative impact excessive technology use is having on young children and their families. While we love technology, we believe it's like any other powerful tool—it must be used with great wisdom.

Parents are wise to set tight limits over the amount of time their children—particularly their little ones—spend watching videos, playing games, etc. This also applies to so-called "educational" videos or games. With our (Charles) youngest child, we decided to limit this to no more than five to ten minutes per day. I can guess what some of you are thinking: "He's just an old dude out of touch with today's world." I may be getting old, but I've never regretted the decision. What this has done for our family is forced us to spend more time interacting and loving on each other. While it's "easier" to let them be entertained by devices, it's far more fulfilling long term to enjoy close relationships.

Too Much Screen Time

- **Increases the odds that children will become addicted**

  Psychologists, therapists, and other mental health professionals are seeing massive numbers of children and teens who are so addicted to screen time they become sullen and aggressive when they don't get it.

- **Interferes with the rapidly growing brain's development of essential neural pathways**

  When children spend their time being entertained, they fail to develop neurons enabling them to develop self-control, delayed gratification, the ability to cope with boredom, and other essential social and emotional skills.

- **Interferes with developing muscles and academic readiness skills**

  Childhood obesity has reached epic proportions. So has the number of children who lack eye-hand and large muscle coordination. Interestingly, such coordination is correlated with children's ability to learn academic skills.

  When little ones learn to throw and catch balls, balance on fallen logs, color with crayons, build with blocks, run after frogs, and other physical activities, they learn the building blocks of cause and effect: When I move a certain way, such and such happens. This cause and effect template helps them later on as they learn that when they put two numbers or letters together, such and such happens.

• Interferes with family bonding

As you'll see in the next chapter, bonding and healthy attachment are everything! You'll also see that such bonding requires eye contact, face-to-face smiles, lots of loving touch, and plenty of meals where healthy food is paired with lots of love and fun. Bonding and attachment also require that basic emotional and physical needs are consistently met by the parent.

Too frequently, children bond with devices more frequently than their parents. Therefore, it's no surprise that so many teens are far more compliant with their electronic devices than with their parents.

Sadly, many adults have also become addicted to their phones and other devices. As a result, they become far more attuned to their screens than the needs of their children. The next time you go to the park or a Little League game, count the number of parents who are watching their phones rather than their children.

As Soon as They Can Spit Food, They're Ready for Love and Logic

Each child is born with an individual temperament and time clock of development. Children learn new skills when they are ready. Toddlers go after independence with the determination of Alexander Hamilton and Patrick Henry. Preschoolers create their own worlds with the imagination of Steve Jobs and Walt Disney. We don't have to be experts in child development to use Love and Logic. We also don't need a degree in child psychology to be a great parent. All we really need to know is that kids are ready for Love and Logic as soon as they're old enough to spit food across the table or crawl away when we're trying to change their diapers.

Love and Logic Experiment #2

Putting an End to Whining

*Teach your child the difference between
a whiney voice and a "big" one.*

The next time your child whines, try saying, "I hear you when your voice sounds big instead of whiney."

Next, have some fun with your child and model the difference between whiney and not whiney.

> "Sweetie, a whiney voice sounds like this, 'I waaaant it. Give it to meeee!' A big voice sounds like, 'Mommy, may I please have this?' I hear big voices, not whiney voices."

When your child begins to whine, go hard of hearing.

When your child begins to whine, pretend you can't hear it. Or say something like, "There's this strange little squeak in my ear. I can't tell what it is. Must be a little buggie or something."

If your child continues to whine, become a broken record.

If your child continues to whine, smile and keep asking, "Why can't I hear you?" Parents are always amazed how fast their kids learn to talk "big."

For an example, review the story of Carter on page 34.

CHAPTER THREE

Planting the Seeds of Responsibility, Kindness, and Empathy

Basic Needs in the Early Years

Have you ever met a child who just didn't seem to care about others? Have you ever met a child who seemed to be missing something down deep in his soul? More and more children are growing up without the basic seeds of responsibility and kindness, and their common missing element is love and empathy for others and themselves. Some of these kids appear troubled, yet quiet and secretive. Others seem ready to explode at any moment. Still others, at first glance, appear perfectly charming, yet prove themselves manipulative and hurtful.

Warning signs in such children become evident early in their lives as we watch them interact with other people. Let's take a look at Joshua as he plays in the backyard.

> Six-year-old Joshua is digging dirt in the yard while his mother plants some flowers. When the telephone rings, his mom goes indoors. As soon as she's out of sight, Josh picks up a rock and throws it through the window of their garage. He's been thinking about doing this for an hour, but his mother's been watching him.

Josh smiles when he hears the crash. Then he dusts off his hands on his pants and goes back to digging. As his mother runs out of the house, she asks him what happened.

"Oliver, from next-door. He threw a rock and broke it," Josh responds with practiced sincerity.

Angry, Joshua's mom rushes back into the house to call Oliver's mother. When she returns to the yard, she's even angrier. "Oliver's mom tells me he isn't home, Josh, and hasn't been home all day."

Joshua responds, "Well, she's lying! I don't know who threw it! If you loved me, you would believe me!" Quietly, he looks down and begins playing again as if nothing has transpired.

Frustrated beyond belief, Mom lectures, "I think you do! Oliver's dad was standing by their dining room window when he saw you throw the rock!"

Joshua looks back and proclaims, "He's lying! I hate him!"

"Did you do it?" Mom asks again. "Why did you do it?" she begs. No answer. Past her limit, she picks him up, takes him into the house, and places him in a chair. Immediately, he bursts into angry tears and begins to scream, "I hate him! I hate you!"

Later in the day, unknown to anyone, Joshua kicks his dog. As it yelps and runs away, Joshua feels a little better.

❤ ❤ ❤

Sadly, there are many Joshuas in the world. His actions are upsetting, because he did what he did on purpose. Afterward, he felt no remorse. When confronted by his mother, he blamed his actions on another child. He even accused an adult of lying. When he was alone again, he took out his rage on the dog.

If they don't get the help they need, the long-term conse-quences for children like Joshua are sad and often tragic. They have difficulty maintaining relationships and lead unsatisfying lives. Those they know become the brunt of ongoing hurt. As they grow up, they often experience a multitude of problems—multiple divorces, illegitimate children, frequent job losses, substance abuse, internet addiction, and so on. In extreme cases, these are the children who go to school and shoot their classmates. These become the teens and young adults who are easily recruited by terrorist groups.

The good news is there is hope for children like Joshua, but only if their parents seek competent professional help as early in the child's life as possible. ◀ There's some even better news. Parents have practical, proven ways of preventing problems like this from happening in the first place—ways of raising responsible, caring kids. Ellie, below, is a good example of this type of child.

> Ellie walks through a neighborhood park with her father. They like to play baseball, and she's learning to be a pitcher. While her dad stops to say hello to a friend, Ellie discovers a collection of rocks near some trees. She picks one up and pitches it as far as she can, to see how far she can throw. Proud of the distance she threw the first, she picks up another and flings away.
>
> As her father continues to visit with his friend, Ellie lets go of still another. Everyone nearby turns to see where the crashing sound came from, and nobody looks at Ellie. To her utter amazement, not to mention terror, she realizes that her arm is stronger than she thought. The park center building now has a broken window.
>
> Embarrassed by her actions, Ellie observes that no one seems to know she threw the rock. Too stunned to speak, she says nothing. Her father notices that she's a little quiet on the way home and obviously has something on her mind. He chalks it up to Ellie being lost in a little girl daydream. He thinks to himself, "Sure glad my kid didn't break that window!"
>
> That night Ellie tosses in her bed. She's unable to fall asleep because of the guilt she feels. She gets out of bed at

two in the morning to wake her father. She stands in his bedroom doorway with tears running down her face.

"Daddy?" she sobs. "I was the one who did it. I broke the window!"

❤ ❤ ❤

What a difference, compared to Joshua. Ellie did not intend to break the window. Instead, she was in one of those experimental modes that kids sometimes get into—wanting to see what happens when you put ketchup in your orange juice, put your feet into your sweatshirt sleeves, or throw a rock as far as you can. Unlike Joshua, who longed to break the window and moved ahead in a devious way, Ellie's action was based on an impulsive thought. She acted on it and was surprised—by her own action as well as by the broken window. Further, Ellie's heart wouldn't allow her to continue deceiving her dad. Unlike Joshua, she felt true remorse.

Ellie and her father reported the accident to the park center. He paid for the repair, and she also agreed to reimburse him by doing extra chores. After working out the payment plan, her father hugged her tightly and said, "That was quite a throw, sweetie. I'm so proud that you were honest. I love you."

Kids like Ellie don't have a war zone rumbling inside them. They experience angry moments like the rest of us, but most of the time they're happy, healthy kids. Furthermore, they're terrible liars. When they try to lie they have a tone in their voices and a look in their eyes that gives them away. They lose sleep and appetite over misbehavior, and deep down, feel really sad about hurting other people or property—even if they don't get caught.

What Makes the Difference between Joshua and Ellie?

What's the difference between a child who cannot sleep at night because of an accident or misbehavior and a child who premeditates destructive actions, doesn't seem to care, blames other people, and apparently suffers no genuine remorse?

**A child's ability to love and respect
oneself and others is primarily determined
by how well that child's basic needs
were met during the first
two years of life.**

We cannot overemphasize the importance of the first years of life. The best way to understand what happens during this time is to, metaphorically speaking, "stand in an infant's shoes"—get inside that child's skin, and lie in that child's crib.

Learning to Trust: The First Two Years of Life

Imagine that you're an infant or very young child, growing up in a healthy family. You're lying in your crib, looking up at the ceiling. From your point of view, life's pretty good.

All of a sudden, you don't feel so good. Life really starts to stink. You've just messed your diaper. You cry out, "Waa! Waa! Waaaaa!" Very soon, somebody comes to look at you. That person picks you up, smiles at you, notices that your diaper is full and changes it. Deep in your soul, you feel, "Life is good! The world is good. I am loved. I can love others."

A few minutes later, you're lying in your crib again, and everything is fine. Minutes later, you get a strange feeling. You feel empty. You're hungry. You cry out. Again, someone comes to look at you. That person picks you up again, smiles at you, figures out that you might want some food, and feeds you. Now you're feeling okay. Life is good again.

Every time an infant's or very young child's basic needs are met, a seed of trust and kindness is planted in that child's mind and heart. On a deep emotional level, a child feels, "Since people are taking such good care of me, I must be really good—and so are they!" In the 1970s, our friend and colleague Dr. Foster Cline described this process in what he termed "The Trust Cycle."

THE TRUST CYCLE STEP #1: *The Child Has a Basic Need*

At the beginning of the cycle, the child has a need—he or she may be hungry, cold, lonely, bored, have a messy diaper, or may be experiencing some other type of pain or discomfort. These are basic needs—the ones that must be addressed for the child's survival. On a deep emotional level, every child knows that he or she will die if these needs are not met. What would you do if you knew you were going to die, but you couldn't walk or speak? Probably what babies and very young children do: scream and cry with all of the rage you could muster.

The Trust Cycle

STEP 1
*The Child has a
Basic Need*

STEP 4
Trust is Achieved

STEP 2
*The Infant Cries
with Rage*

STEP 3
The Need is Fulfilled

THE TRUST CYCLE STEP #2: *The Infant Cries with Rage*

As the infant or very young child lying in the crib, you begin to scream, kick, and cry. "I'm going to die if somebody doesn't come to take care of me," you realize. "This is a life-and-death matter!"

THE TRUST CYCLE STEP #3: *The Need Is Fulfilled*

Suddenly, somebody comes along, smiles at you, sniffs you, picks you up, finds out what's wrong, and finally feeds you or meets some other need. As this happens, you receive the basic components of human bonding—eye contact, smiles, touch, and relief from pain or discomfort.

Basic Emotional Components of Bonding
- Eye contact
- Smiles
- Hugs, holding, and touch
- Relief from pain and discomfort

Just as food is essential to keep your baby alive, so are all the emotional nutrients of bonding. For over a half-century, scientists have documented that infants who receive no eye contact, no smiles, and no hugging or holding will die. "Failure to thrive" is the classic term for this tragic condition.

**An infant will die without food,
but also may die without eye contact,
smiles, and touch.**

More recently, research has documented that young children who consistently experience emotional nurturing have healthier brains than those who do not.

Nurture creates neurons!

The first time you make eye contact with your child and both of you explore the magical appearance of the other, one of your child's unspoken needs is satisfied. Just as a picture is worth a thousand words, so is a look. By looking into your baby's eyes and allowing your child to look into yours, wordless communication takes place.

A smile speaks volumes about how you feel about your child. From the very beginning, your baby recognizes you and smiles to acknowledge attachment to you. The child who sees smiles learns how to smile, and every time you share one, the bond grows. The child develops a smile in his or her heart.

Before birth and beyond, the sound of your heartbeat, your physical connection, and your warmth give your child a sense of security and trust. When this is missing early in life, children harden. Their hearts close to themselves and others, and they begin to believe that the only way to survive is to dominate or hurt others.

THE TRUST CYCLE STEP #4: *Trust Is Achieved*

As you are being fed, cleaned, held, etc., you feel, "Oh, what a relief! This person just saved my life! This is a good world I live in. People can be trusted to take care of me. I must really be loved! I'm free to love others." If we are able to love, it's only because we were first loved by someone else.

Infants who know their basic needs are going to be met, develop love and kindness in their hearts. Those who don't, spend their lives angry at the world and themselves.

As each cycle ends and a child's need is realized, a notch of trust is etched into their being. The trust cycle goes round and round many times in the course of a day, a week, a year. Every time it's completed, the child develops a stronger level of trust—not only in the caregiver, but also in society. Simply stated, an infant's first human relationship strongly shapes how he or she views the world. When we have a basic feeling of trust toward society, we tend to live by its laws, morals, and ethics. When we lack this trust, we do whatever we can to undermine core values—we lie, steal, cheat, hurt, and even kill.

Broken Trust

In more and more families today, there are significant breaks taking place in the trust cycle. The reasons, many and varied, are sometimes within a parent's control and sometimes not:

1. Abuse and neglect.
2. One or both of the child's parents have alcohol, drug, internet, video game, cell phone, or other addictions.
3. One or both of the child's parents suffer from serious depression or some other form of mental illness.
4. The child's parents are injured, killed, or become very ill—in war, or a personal disaster.
5. The child has an illness that the parents want to cure, but can't.
6. The child has been adopted or placed in foster care after failing to be cared for properly.
7. The child has spent most of his or her first months of life in poor quality daycare.

Uncaring or emotionally troubled parents aren't the only ones who may have kids with these problems. Some families have children who were born with an illness. In these cases, loving parents want to take away the child's pain, but can't figure out what's wrong. By the time a child gets to the doctor, perhaps months later, the child has felt, over and over again, that the world is a painful place.

Breaks in the Trust Cycle

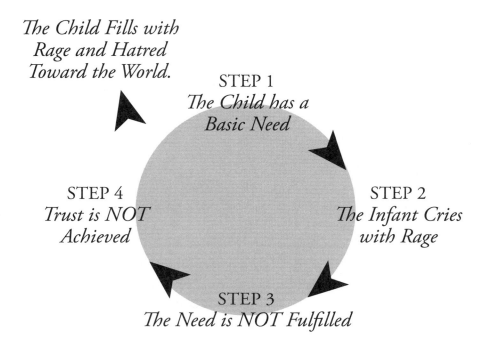

The Child Fills with Rage and Hatred Toward the World.

STEP 1
The Child has a Basic Need

STEP 4
Trust is NOT Achieved

STEP 2
The Infant Cries with Rage

STEP 3
The Need is NOT Fulfilled

Consequences of Breaks in the Cycle

The major consequence of a chronic, ongoing break in the Trust Cycle is "down-to-the-marrow-of-the-bones" rage. This child is angry at the world—feels betrayed. "What kind of world is this? Nobody is going to take care of me. I hate this place!"

**A child who reaches this point, makes an unconscious decision.
"From now on, I'm going to hurt people before they hurt me!"**

Some Consequences of Significant Breaks in the Trust Cycle
- Excessive anger and rage
- Destructiveness
- Chronic lying
- Lack of remorse
- Poor problem-solving skills
- Cruelty to animals
- Lots of pain for everyone 🔊

The consequences of chronic breaks in the trust cycle during a child's first year of life can take a heavy toll on parents, as well as on the child. Kids who are filled with rage have trouble functioning in the healthy ways that most of us take for granted. Since they don't see themselves in a positive light, they cannot see the rest of the world that way either. Life is painful for these kids, and for everyone around them.

If you are taking the time to read this book, we're assuming you're a loving person who tends to your children's needs and responds to them with consistency. Occasionally, even the most loving and committed parent errs and fails to meet a need. An occasional miss is not going to scar our kids for life. Nobody is perfect. Serious problems develop when basic needs are unmet on a *chronic* and *ongoing* basis.

All we really need to understand is that wise parents do whatever they can to meet their young children's needs. They smile, they hold, they rock, they gaze into their children's eyes, and they prove that people can be trusted. If the child continues to cry and cannot be soothed, wise parents consult with a qualified medical professional.

The Difference between Needs and Wants

Over the years, there have been some books in the marketplace suggesting that parents should let their infants "cry it out." Those of us who value what Love and Logic has to teach believe that parents who allow their infant to "cry it out"—who do not respond to their baby's basic needs—create serious breaks in the trust cycle. Some of these books may be confusing kids' needs with kids' wants. Let's take a look at the difference.

It seems obvious that when children become adults, they still have a need for food, water, and shelter. Less obvious is that we all continue to need unconditional love, a sense of belonging, feelings of self-competence, and a healthy realization of control. These are *basic needs*, and as we grow, they remain fairly constant.

As infants become toddlers, they also develop a wide array of desires. As Foster Cline says, "A two-year-old is not only a bundle of needs, but now is a bundle of wants."

**We all have difficulty,
from time to time, telling the difference
between our needs and our wants.**

As adults we may think we "need" a new sports car—or the very latest tablet or phone. We may believe we "need" to win a million dollars. Do you have any friends who believe they "need" to take constant selfies and post them online?

A child may declare a "need" for the latest laptop, a new bike, or the video game that "everyone else has." In truth, we—and our kids—don't need these things. We want them. People who can't tell the difference tend to lead painful lives. They have money and relationship problems, and they're chronically unhappy. Since the first edition of this book, entitlement among youth—and adults—has reached epidemic proportions. Why? Largely because we as a society have failed to help our children understand the difference between needs and wants.

**Children who grow up believing
they are entitled to everything they desire
serve a life sentence of unhappiness
and resentment. Nothing is ever good enough.**

Meeting Needs and Limiting Wants

When it comes to toddlers and preschoolers, our responsibility as parents is to accomplish three tasks:

- **Consistently meet basic needs.** We complete the trust cycle and provide our children with the essentials they need for a kind, loving heart. This means that when our child under the age of one year cries, we don't worry about "spoiling" them. We swoop in and do our best to rescue them from their discomfort.

- **Distinguish between kids' needs and wants.** As they pass their first birthday, we begin to show our kids that there's a difference between what they need and what they want. ◀))

- **Set limits.** For the rest of their childhood and teen years, we continue to meet basic needs while setting limits on their "wants."

As the second year of life approaches, the role we play as parents must adapt. To maintain the parent-child bond, we must also begin setting limits on wants. Does every child yearn down deep for the love and security of firm limits? Absolutely!

Unfortunately, many parents believe that if they give their children free rein—allow them to do anything they want—their kids will be happy and will grow into responsible, loving adults. Nothing could be further from the truth.

As we now know, to become kind and responsible people, kids must develop a healthy bond with the adults who care for them. What is often forgotten is that this bond can only be maintained when loving limits are regularly set and faithfully enforced. Why? Limits say to your child:

- "I love you enough to keep you safe."
- "I love you enough to help you feel secure."
- "I care enough to teach you the difference between your needs and wants."
- "I care enough to prepare you for the real world."

Healthy bonding requires both love and limits.

If you've ever seen a child who is considered "bossy"—like Jake who kept his mother hopping on their camping trip—you've seen the result of failing to set and enforce enough limits at a young age. Although Jake may appear to be in control of his mother, down deep he is feeling totally out of control. His little subconscious mind is probably wondering, "If Mommy can't control me, who will keep me safe? Why doesn't she love me enough to set some limits?"

The Irony of Setting Too Few Limits

Isn't it ironic that kids whose parents fail to set and enforce limits feel unloved and angry? Although they tend to test and protest, we have learned over and over again that limits are what kids really want. Invariably, when we talk with out-of-control teenagers or adults who were juvenile delinquents and lucky enough to survive, we ask them, "If you could go back to when you were a child, what would you change?" most of them say something like, "I wish my parents had reeled me in when I was a kid. Why didn't they make me behave?"

A counselor we know sat down with a teenager who'd led a pretty rough life. She had been promiscuous, had become pregnant, and was in trouble with the law. She went on to describe how she had smoked pot and guzzled beer with her dad as a ten-year-old. When the counselor asked her what she thought about it, her eyes lit up with rage and she said, "I hate him!" Surprised, the counselor said, "You had so much freedom. Why do you hate your father?"

Even more surprised, the teen responded, "I hate him 'cause he let me do anything I wanted. He never made me behave. Look at me now!"

Limits Teach Kids How to Say "No"

We all want our kids to say "no" to drugs, alcohol, texting while driving, meeting people they've met online, etc. How will they learn to say "no" when they never hear it from us? As teens, many of us made a solemn commitment to never become like our parents. When we aged into adulthood, guess what happened? Most of us became very much like our parents. I (Charles) feel very blessed by this! Modeling is our most powerful parenting tool. When we apply Love and Logic, we show what it looks like to remain loving, self-controlled people who know when it's wise to say "no." All great leaders know that what we do is far more important than what we say.

Limits Contribute to Creativity and School Success

Most parents accept that we don't help our toddlers and preschoolers when we give them too much freedom. Still, they remain concerned about putting a lid on a child's personality or individuality. If we lead with too strong a hand—set too many limits—will we put a damper on some creative aspect of our child, burying it forever? Will we frighten our kids away from being free to express who they really are?

At Love and Logic conferences we have told thousands of parents:

> **If you want your children to have
> internal controls and inner freedom,
> you must first provide them with
> external controls.**

A child who is given boundaries, and choices within those boundaries, is actually freer to be creative, inventive, active, and insightful. Why? Brain science has demonstrated that the creative portions of our brain only operate at full capacity when we feel safe and secure. A brain concerned with a lack of secure boundaries and unpredictability will focus most of its energy on meeting those needs. A relaxed brain with these and other needs met has energy to learn, grow, and create new and exciting ideas.

When children experience chronic difficulty learning at school, the root cause often involves a lack of limits, structure, and predictability at home. In my (Charles's) book, "From Bad Grades to a Great Life," I discuss the reasons for this and note that intrinsic motivation is heavily dependent upon the calming impact of loving limits.

> **The world is full of limits within which
> we all must live.
> Give your children a gift. Teach them how
> to be creative within these limits.**

Love and Logic Experiment #3

Strengthening the Bond

**Pay attention to what your child loves
and write these things down.**

Over the course of a week, pay close attention to what your child really loves the very most. Here are some typical examples:

- A certain stuffed animal or toy
- Drawing or coloring

- Playing a certain fantasy game, such as "princess" or "super hero"
- A certain shirt, pair of shoes, or pair of pants
- A silly word or saying
- A specific type of food
- Playing catch

At least three times a week, walk over to your child, smile, and notice these interests.

On one day, you may say something like, "I noticed you like to draw." Two days later you may say, "I noticed you really love those sneakers." A day or two later you might say, "I noticed you like to play good guys and bad guys."

DO NOT end these statements with something like, "That's great!"

Why do we say this? Over the past twenty years, we have found that kids almost always respond best if we can avoid adding any type of judgment to our noticing. Why? Many children seem to reason, "If she thinks this is great, maybe she will think the next thing I do is not great."

Our primary goal here is to show that we notice our children's interests rather than judging these interests as either good or bad.

Notice how your child reacts.

Most parents are really amazed how well this little "noticing" routine works. They often say things like, "My daughter just beams with joy when I do this." They also comment that their children are typically more compliant when they've been using this tool. Why is this so? When children feel that their parents notice and value their interests, they are always happier and more cooperative.

CHAPTER FOUR

Love Them Enough to Take Care of Yourself

Parenting Doesn't Have to Be Complicated

Parents often feel overwhelmed because they've been led to believe that they have to be experts in child development in order to raise responsible, healthy kids.

Hogwash! In our Love and Logic approach, we encourage parents to avoid overcomplicating their lives with complex theories or techniques. What's our advice to you? Keep it simple and have some fun.

**Effective parenting is achieved when parents
learn a few simple tools so well that they can pull them off
with a smile on their face and no sweat on their brow.**

Over the last four decades, we've come to realize that the four basic principles you learned in Chapter 1 apply to all ages, from little babies to adults. Rather than rethink parenting for each age, the goal of this book is to give you specific examples of how to apply each of these principles with young children. The goal of this book is to make your life easier—not harder.

The Two Rules of Love and Logic

The Love and Logic approach can be boiled down to two simple rules for adults:

RULE #1:
Remain a healthy role model. Do this by setting limits and taking care of yourself in loving, unselfish ways.

RULE #2:
Turn every mistake or misbehavior into a learning opportunity. Do this by providing sincere empathy before allowing your child to learn from the consequences.

That's it. When we begin to experiment with these rules, we're quickly on our way toward becoming the best parents we can be— and also having a lot more fun with our kids. In this chapter and the next, we will learn more about Rule #1. In Chapter 6, we'll get better acquainted with Rule #2. Sit back, relax, and get ready for a life with lower blood pressure and happier, more responsible kids.

THE FIRST RULE OF LOVE AND LOGIC

Remain a healthy role model by taking good care of yourself in unselfish ways.

- Replace frustration, anger, or sarcasm with sincere empathy.
- Replace threats and warnings with simple actions.
- Set limits you can enforce.
- Share the control you don't need.

The first rule of Love and Logic parenting, with children of any age, involves providing limits in loving ways. When we make a child aware of our limits, and do it in a caring way, we take good care of ourselves and model healthy behavior.

Anger, Frustration, or Sarcasm

Many of us have been taught that we get kids to behave by angrily laying down the law. That's how some of our parents operated, and so did many of their parents before them. In the "good old days," these techniques often seemed to work. Have times ever changed. In today's society, parents are seeing over and over that anger and frustration actually make the problem worse. In fact, nothing seems to make a sour behavior stick better than an entertaining display of parental frustration and anger.

Isn't it amazing? After all this time, it turns out that getting frustrated and angry gets us the exact opposite of what we want. Take a look at Alex and his mother as they sit in the airport.

It's late in the evening, and four-year-old Alex is tired and bored. He and his mom are waiting for a commuter flight. He's saying, "I want to go to Grandma's now! I hate this place! It sucks!"

His mother is tired, too, and frustrated. She says, "You stop saying that! It's not nice! Cut that out! Stop it right now, young man!"

Alex pinches her. She responds immediately with more anger. "You pinched me? We don't do that! We treat each other with respect around here! That's one!" The kid continues to misbehave. "That's two!" his mother says. "Alex! Don't you do that again!" When he does, she takes him into the restroom and spanks him.

A minute later, Alex emerges from the bathroom with his mother. Snot is running out of his nose, and his face is red as a tomato. When they sit down again, Alex continues his meltdown. The more frustrated and angry Mommy gets, the more monster-like Alex becomes.

Saved by the boarding announcement, Alex and his mother board the plane, which is half-empty. They sit right behind a businessman who is trying to complete some work on his laptop. Within minutes, Alex starts to kick the back of this poor gentleman's seat.

The man turns around and calmly says to the mother, "Can you please do something about your child? He's kicking the back of my seat."

The pent-up and upset mother gives the man a look of exasperation and says, "What do you expect me to do?"

Ten minutes later, Alex is still kicking away. Really irritated now, the man stands up and finds that the seat behind Alex is empty. Now the tables are turned, and this grown man is kicking the back of the boy's seat.

The mother turns around and says, "What are you doing?"

With all of the sarcasm he can muster, the businessman responds, "What do you expect me to do? I can't help it."

❤ ❤ ❤

The Misbehavior Cycle

It's easy to laugh at the story of Alex and his mommy because it's happening to somebody else. But wait! What if the tables are turned, and we are the ones in the parental hot seat?

First of all, let's cut Mom—and ourselves—some slack. She's doing the best she can under very, very difficult circumstances. We'd also like to admit that all of us blow it from time to time. I (Charles) often joke, "I used to be a parenting 'expert.' This is, until I had kids." Airplanes and kids are often a difficult combo. Sometimes I even encourage parents to resort to bribery just to make it through the trip. As long as we're not making it a habit, promising ice cream cones or some other treat is okay if it will save our sanity and that of everyone around. Just don't promise 'em a pony.

Let's get back to the subject of frustration and anger. When a parent displays these emotions and threatens their child—and the child continues to misbehave—what has the parent achieved? More importantly, what is their child learning? Here's what happens.

The Misbehavior Cycle

STEP 1
*Child Experiments
with
Misbehavior*

STEP 4
*Child Begins to
Feel Hopeless*

STEP 2
*Parent Gets Frustrated,
Angry, or Sarcastic*

STEP 3
*Child Develops Disrespect
for Authority Figures*

THE MISBEHAVIOR CYCLE STEP #1:
Child Experiments with Misbehavior

Every child is going to experiment with misbehavior. In fact, the healthiest little children are those who act like young scientists. These little Einsteins run experiments to see how the world works. They decide, based on analyzing the results of their research, how they want to live their lives. In their little subconscious minds, they seem to do a lot of pondering: "I wonder what would happen if...?"

"I wonder what will happen if I spit food across the table? I wonder what's going to happen if I lie down while I'm shopping with my mom and start to scream 'I want it. I want it!'" Some of the experiments are sour, and some are sweet. "I wonder what will happen if I say please or give Mommy a hug. I wonder what will happen if I just sit here and quietly eat my food?"

THE MISBEHAVIOR CYCLE STEP #2:
Parent Gets Frustrated, Angry, or Sarcastic

The best way to create a "mad scientist" rather than a marvelous one is to display frustrated anger or sarcasm when your child misbehaves. Remember, anger and frustration feed misbehavior. It's often easy to forget this and start the lectures: "Don't you do that! That's not nice. That's one! That's two! That's two and one-half! That's fifteen and three-quarters!"

Soon the child hears the dreaded parental, "I mean it!"— which actually says to the kid, "I'm totally out of skills, and I have no idea what I'm going to do with you!" No wonder kids often grin when they hear these words.

THE MISBEHAVIOR CYCLE STEP #3:
The Child Develops Disrespect for Authority Figures

Sadly, the child looks up at the adult, and on a subconscious level, begins to believe some rather unfortunate things:

- "Wow! Look at this. The most powerful people in my life can't make me behave." The child develops a perception of authority figures as easily frustrated and easy to push around. Sadly, this belief can last a lifetime and create major pain for everyone, particularly the child.

- "Hey! It's really entertaining to see big people ticked off!" Have you ever known people who've made a hobby out of frustrating their teachers, boss, police officers, or spouse? What a bummer! Just pray someone like this never buys the house next-door.

THE MISBEHAVIOR CYCLE STEP #4:
The Child Begins to Feel Hopeless

How must a child begin to feel when nobody is able in a loving way to make him or her behave? Consider the following:

> **"If the most powerful people in my life**
> **can't make me behave, and they're all bigger**
> **and older than I am,**
> **I must be pretty bad—really bad and**
> **pretty hopeless."**

Using frustration, anger, or sarcasm is one of the quickest ways to make children develop a negative view of authority figures—and then, themselves. When kids feel bad about themselves, hopelessness soon follows—"Why should I even try when I'm so bad?"

> **Sense of Self = Behavior = Sense of Self**
> **Children act according to how we see them,**
> **and they see themselves according to**
> **how they act.**

When kids have a healthy sense of self, the odds go up in favor of their behaving well. Think about it for a moment. Are you ever around someone who just plain believes in you? It rubs off on you, doesn't it? And don't you find that you're nearly always your best around that person? Like us, kids rise to the occasion when they feel good about the positive things they can achieve.

In contrast, have you ever noticed what it's like to be around someone who's constantly critical? How do you act around them? Do you find yourself actually living down to their expectations? Do you ever find yourself giving them the very worst you have to offer?

Breaking the Cycle

How do we prevent or break the misbehavior cycle? Simply put, we show our kids that we can handle them without breaking a sweat. We replace anger and frustration with soft words and powerful, yet kind, actions.

If they can handle me that easy, I must be okay!

Let's take a look at how one Love and Logic parent proved this to his young son.

> I (Charles) watched a father and son as they did a bit of shopping in our local grocery store. Let's call them Logan and Zack. Logan is toddling behind his father, Zack. Soon the tot is gravitating toward everything on the shelves. "I want this. I want this. I want that." Before long, he's sitting in the middle of the aisle playing with objects he's pulled off the shelves.
>
> Some parents might stop right there and say, "Stop that right now!" or, "You put that back on the shelf! Come on! Come on!" But Zack doesn't break a sweat. He keeps moving and walks around the corner where Logan can't see him, but he can see Logan. Giggling as he peeks around the corner, Dad watches his sweet little boy.
>
> Suddenly the air is pierced with screams as Logan realizes he might be "lost."
>
> "Daddy? Daddy? Daddy! Daaaaa—deeeee!" he yells, running down the aisle. Seeing his son rounding the corner, Zack continues down the aisle, smiling and saying, "Hey, Logan, little buddy! Good to see you again! I was wondering if you were going to catch up with me today. It sure would be sad for you if you got lost." ◀)
>
> What's Zack doing? Is he showing little Logan that he can handle him without breaking a sweat? What's this little

one learning? He's learning his job—which is to keep up with Dad. Too frequently we send the message to our children that it's our job to keep up with them while in public. Zack's actions communicated that it was his son's job to keep up with him. Do actions speak louder than words?

**When we parent without
showing frustration, anger, or sarcasm,
the odds for success increase
in a very big way.**

Love and Logic Experiment #4

Have Some Fun with Temper Tantrums

Tantrum-tamer #1: Keep on truckin'.

The next time your child has a tantrum in the store, keep on truckin'. That's right. Walk away, turn the corner, and peek around it. Make sure your child can't see you. Most kids will suddenly realize you aren't going to hang around for their fits, and they'd better keep up.

For a fun example of this approach, review the story of little Logan on page 76.

By the way, this same technique works at home, too.

Tantrum-tamer #2: Encourage the art form.

A second strategy for taming tantrums is to encourage the art form. When your child begins a meltdown, put a bored look on your face and say, "Nice tantrum, but I think you are losing your touch. Last time you screamed a lot louder and kicked your feet a lot harder. I'm really disappointed. Show me how it's really done. Give me your best. Come on."

A friend of ours routinely used this approach with her son. With a smile on her face, she recounted one day when she begged her son to have a fit. How did he respond? With both hands on his hips and a twisted little face, he said, "No! I don't want to!"

CHAPTER FIVE

Give Your Children an Advantage in Life

The Way the Real World Works

Love and Logic is devoted to helping parents raise kids who are prepared for the real world. What does this mean? Like frustration and anger, which get us nothing but more of the same, threats and repeated warnings do not prepare our kids for real-life situations. I (Charles) got a strong grip on this concept as I drove to the airport one day.

Finally I had a car with less than 300,000 miles on the odometer. It even had a CD player instead of a cassette deck. I was speeding down the freeway, looking more at the CD player than the road, when I glanced up just in time to see a tire fly off of a truck and land right in front of me. What was I to do? I couldn't go left. I couldn't go right. I couldn't stop in time. All I could do was grit my teeth and hope for the best.

I pulled to the side of the road and got out of the car. Quickly surveying the damage, I noticed oil all over the road. Then I saw the interesting collection of car parts decorating the highway behind me. What a drag! Immediately my brain began surging, "What do I do now? I'm going to miss my flight. Then I'm going to miss my meeting in Omaha. Then I might lose my job." Thank goodness for cell phones. Calling my office, I begged for a quick ride to the airport—and a tow truck.

It was close, but I actually made my flight. In my hotel room that night, I tried to get some sleep. As I closed my eyes, the inside of my eyelids became television sets. What did I see? The entire incident kept replaying itself over and over again in my head—the tire flying out of control, hitting it, the oil on the road, my heart racing, etc. It occurred to me that there had to be a reason why this experience was burned so deeply in my subconscious mind. There had to be some reason why this event had such a great impact on me. All I knew at the moment was that I was never again going to watch the dash more carefully than the road.

Why will I never forget this lesson? Is it because the accident happened so quickly? Was it because the experience was scary? Was it possibly because the tire came without warning? Is this often how consequences work in the real world? Are children better prepared to make good decisions about big issues when they understand there aren't always warnings or second chances? Wise parents understand that the more warnings and reminders they give their children, the more warnings and reminders their children will come to need.

Or—has my memory failed me about this event? Did a state trooper pull up alongside me as I was driving down the highway and yell out his window, "You'd better pay attention to the road, because a tire might shred off of a big rig and land right in front of you! That's one!"?

Did he roll up his window, move on, and let me go? Did I then get stopped by a sheriff, a mile down the road, who warned, "I've been talking to the state trooper back there, and you haven't been paying attention! You better stop that right now! We really mean it this time. That's two!"?

Farther down the road, did the chief of police drive up and say, "That's two-and-a-half! We really do mean it this time!"? Of course not!

❤ ❤ ❤

Real-World Consequences Often Happen without Warning

It may be argued that we have a population of citizens who are addicted to warnings. When they don't get enough, they sue. I (Jim) realized we were in big trouble as a culture when a woman sued a mall for failing to warn her that she might fall into their fountain if she wasn't paying attention. This grown woman—so engrossed with her texting—walked directly into a wall with such force that she flipped into the pool. She quickly sued for emotional pain and suffering due to the extreme embarrassment. Because her embarrassment was so severe, she made an appearance on multiple daytime TV talk shows to describe it. Huh?

Do we want to raise kids with a strong sense of personal responsibility, or do we want to create ones who blame others for their misdeeds? Do we want to raise kids with a strong sense of cause and effect, or ones with a very distorted one?

Is it possible that we give kids an inaccurate and potentially dangerous perspective on cause and effect when we warn them two, three, or four times before enforcing limits? By giving them all these warnings, do we plant a seed in their minds that can influence them to reason, "I really don't have to worry much about making careful decisions—nothing bad will happen until I'm warned at least two times"?

Our children are better prepared for life when they understand that the consequences of poor choices can happen without warning.

How might a child who's been raised with repeated warnings deal with peer pressure to try drugs, have sex, shoplift, visit porn sites, participate in cyber bullying, etc.? Sadly, it's quite probable that he or she might reason, "Well, something bad might happen, but not right away. In fact, I can probably do drugs and have sex at least two times before anything bad really happens."

When we wrote the first edition of this book fifteen years ago, employers were sharing their frustrations regarding finding employees who were able to complete duties without being nagged. Are you guessing this problem has diminished or intensified? Far too many employees—even highly educated professionals— require massive handholding. If they get reprimanded or fired, they say childish things like, "You didn't warn me! You only mentioned this once. I didn't think you really wanted me to do that. You didn't tell me that I couldn't play video games during work hours. Not fair!"

Learning to Make Wise Decisions—the First Time

We want our kids to have two major thoughts about the decisions they make:

- "Life's pretty good. People are kind to me and meet my needs. But if I make a poor decision, something bad could happen, and I'd have no warning."

- "Every decision I make is important. I wonder how this one's going to affect the rest of my life?"

Kids who think in this way have a fighting chance against peer pressure. Spared threats and repeated warnings, they quickly learn to make wise decisions—the first time. Wouldn't it be nice if our kids could start learning this as soon as possible?

Set the Limit Once and Follow Through

Young parents sometimes use warnings because they love their kids and they have read pop psychology books that tell them to do so. Love and Logic parents do not warn their children two, three, or four times before imposing a consequence. They set the limit once—and follow through with loving yet powerful actions.

Instead of saying, "Pick up your toys…" and then saying, "Oh, now, didn't I tell you to pick up your toys?" and then warning, "If you don't pick up your toys, I'm going to have to… ," the Love and Logic parent simply says, "Feel free to keep the toys you pick up!"

That's it. Once is enough. Then, when the toys are still there, the parent says, "Oh, how sad," picks up the toys, and doesn't return them until the child has earned them back by doing some small chores or helping the parent in some other way. Using this approach, how long is it going to take for the child to get really good at picking up toys? If we teach our kids that sad things can happen when wise decisions aren't made the first time, will they be happier and far safer in the long run? One thing is certain. Their future bosses will love them…and so will their spouses.

**Set limits once and follow through
with loving actions instead of warnings.
Teach them how to make wise decisions the first time.**

The key to success involves setting the limit once—following through with action. That's right. The most successful parents use very few words when things are going wrong. Instead they focus on providing a quick dose of empathy as they enforce the limits. Then they follow through in loving yet firm ways.

How Do We "Set the Limit Once"?

It's easy to *say*, "Set the limit once," but how do we actually do it? With very young kids, we fall back on the "Three L's." Real estate brokers will often note that the value of any given property depends on three things: Location—location—location. The same goes for setting and enforcing limits with very young children:

Our Location

Sometimes parents find it most effective to say, "I will play with you (or read to you, help you with your hair, etc.) when you are acting nice."

When their child starts to act nasty, they empathetically sing, "Uh-oh. This is so sad. We can try this again when you're ready to act sweet." Then they move away and allow their child time to calm down and think.

The Location of the Problem Object

Other times parents find it wiser to say, "You may play with this truck (or any other object) as long you are doing so nicely." When the object isn't being shared, it makes contact with the dog, or is used for any other form of mayhem, the parent empathetically sings, "Uh-oh. This is so sad," and they quickly remove the object.

The Child's Location

Under other circumstances, parents find it most effective to say, "Sweetie, you may stay with us as long as you are acting sweet." Let's imagine that little Tiffany is spitting and throwing her carrots rather than eating them. Acting quickly, her mommy removes her from the highchair while singing, "Uh-oh. This is sad. It looks like dinner is over."

The "Uh-Oh" Song: Training Little Ones to Listen

Many years ago, I (Charles) developed a powerful yet loving strategy for training small children to behave. I'd like to say that I did so out of completely unselfish motives. Honestly, my prime desire was to find something that might work with our first little boy.

When our beloved Marky reached the wise age of sixteen months, he'd decided that he was now "big." This meant—at least in his own mind—that he could do all things without being helped. All day long I'd hear things like, "No! I open the door! No! Me eat! No! I put shirt on! No! Me flush poo-poo! No! I feed dog."

Breakfast was one of the things he desperately wanted to do by himself and for himself. I decided that since I was going to be home, I would put an old, worn-out shower curtain on the floor, give him a bowl of warm mush and let him go at it. If he dropped any on the shower curtain, I could fling it out in the backyard afterward, and everyone would be happy, including the dog.

I also thought, "While he's eating, I'll have time to go in the other room and shave. This is great!" As soon as my face was covered with messy lather, I heard the sound. What was it? Outrageous giggling and laughter flowing from the dining room.

Arriving on the scene, what did I see? Oh the horror! There was little Marky, giggling wildly as he slapped the pool of mush he'd poured on his tray. There was Lady, the cocker spaniel, wearing a bowl of the warm cereal as a hat.

Her long tongue licked away at the mess, and her short tail wagged with joy. She was deliriously happy. Marky was deliriously happy. I was not happy! Have you ever had fantasies about the "behavior management" techniques you'd really like to use with your kids?

I took a deep breath and gave myself a quick talking to: "Handle this without breaking a sweat. That's the main thing. Instead of getting frustrated and angry, show him how calm and collected you can be. Make it look easy!"

So, I looked at Marky and sang the "Uh-Oh Song." What's the "Uh-Oh Song"?

"Uh-oh! This is so sad. Looks like a little bedroom time."

Then I gently carried him off to his bedroom for some "recovery time." ◆)

Before we continue with the story, please let me be clear about something. If little Marky had accidentally bumped his bowl off the table, then I would have simply asked him to help me clean it up. No big deal. This, however, was clearly not an accident. This wonderful little guy had recently taken up the fine art of food flinging. Like any self-respecting toddler, he was experimenting and testing limits big time.

Let's get back to the story. Arriving in his room, I placed him on his bed and said, "You may come out of your room as soon as you're acting sweet. Do you need the door open, or the door shut?"

His answer included plenty of screaming and a flying teddy bear aimed at my head. In toddler talk this means, "Daddy, I need my door shut." As I left, I had to remind myself, "Don't say a word. Keep your mouth shut." As I closed the door, I heard him scream, "Mommy! I want my mommy! Grandma! Grandma! Mommy! Lady! Laaadeee!" As you probably remember, Lady was the name of our dog.

❤ ❤ ❤

When parents place their child in the bedroom, how do they ensure that the door remains shut? Simple, commonsense solutions are usually the best. We can remove the handle, turn the door around so the lock is on the outside, or stuff the top of the door with a towel, making it a bit more difficult for the child to open. Of course, we remain just outside the door, carefully monitoring the situation. The basic rule of thumb is this: The child stays in the room until he or she is calm. Then we wait a minute or two, for ourselves. ◆)

When this time comes, we enter the room, give them a loving hug and say, "Sweetie, I love you. That was so sad." Then we go on with our lives. Do not fall into the trap of lecturing your child about what he or she should learn. Why? Because doing so in essence says to your child, "You're not very smart, are you? You can't figure this out by yourself. How sad."

Save Most of the Attention for Happy Times

Some parents ask, "Why do you use the room? Why don't you just put him in the corner or on a chair?"

The reason we use a room rather than asking a child to stay in the corner or on a chair is because many of us have a difficult time doing this without a red face and lots of words. Often the child starts talking, crying, or trying to leave, and the parent goes over and gives the child too much pizzazz: "You stay there! Don't leave! I told you to stay put! I mean it." Remember: Anger and frustration feed misbehavior.

**The best way to raise a chronically unhappy
and poorly behaved kid
is to make a habit of giving them a lot of attention
or pizzazz when they are misbehaving.** ◀ᐧ

The nice thing about the room is that you can take your child there, latch the door, stay right outside the room, and avoid a major control battle. The key is making sure you don't say anything to your child through the door. Remember, wise parents give their kids plenty of attention when they are acting sweet and little or no attention when they are acting sour.

**What message do we want to send our children?
"Sweetheart, the way you get lots of attention in this house
is by behaving and by being nice."**

Or…

**"The way you get no attention in this house is by
throwing fits and acting nasty."**

Steps for the "Uh-Oh Song"

Since the "Uh-Oh Song" is such a powerful tool with very young kids, we like to make sure we always teach it well. How about a review of the important "Uh-Oh Song" steps? Parents who've mastered them always tell us how much happier their families have become.

1. **Use this only up to approximately age four.** The "Uh-Oh Song" is designed for children small enough to carry safely. It's also designed for little ones who aren't quite old enough to do a bit more complex thinking or problem solving. Once your children reach three or four years of age, begin transitioning toward using the really fun techniques in chapters 6 and 7.

   Interestingly, parents who've been consistent with the "Uh-Oh Song" early in their children's lives find that when the kids are older, singing "uh-oh" still has an effect. Even as a teen, my (Charles's) son Marc would often shape up his behavior when he'd hear it. Of course, when he didn't, I shied away from carrying him to his room.

2. **Instead of making threats or giving warnings, sing, "Uh-oh" and take action.** Maybe you'll carry your child into the bedroom and say, "Looks like a little bedroom time." Or maybe you'll take away an offending object and say calmly, "All gone!" Whatever action you take begins with "uh-oh!" Why? Because singing this simple song really communicates, "You are such a great kid, and I am such a great parent that I can handle you without yelling, without frowning, and without stressing myself out." Parents also tell us that singing, "uh-oh" helps them stay calm.

   Please note. This technique is not for infants and very young children who are crying or acting out because they have a need that must be fulfilled. When a child has a basic need, meet it instead of punishing or ignoring the child! Remember the trust cycle? The "Uh-Oh Song" is designed to limit children's wants, not deprive them of what they need.

3. **Gently lead or carry your child to his or her room.** Make the room safe ahead of time. Wise parents remove anything they don't want broken.

4. **Give your child a choice about the door.** "Do you need the door shut, or open?" If a child comes out before she's ready, then shut the door and make sure it stays shut. Turn the lock around. Put a towel on top of the door; wedge it tightly so she can't pull it open. Put a latch on the outside. Whatever's safe and easily done. Remember to stay just outside the door.

5. **Say, "Feel free to come out when you're acting sweet."** Don't let your child out until she's calm. Some kids need temporarily extended time limits. With some children, the first few times this technique is used, they will need to be in the room for more than an hour. It's okay if a parent checks from time to time, but a kid really needs to stay in there until she's ready to behave. Parents using this technique tell us that the time required begins to shorten very quickly if they remain consistent. They say things like, "The first couple of days were really hard. Then she rarely needed to go to her room or spend much time there. It's great! What a different kid."

   Most children quickly learn that misbehavior doesn't pay. There may be an initial period of drama, but that behavior usually starts to diminish rather rapidly—as long as parents don't interact with a child while he or she is in the room. Remember, the best way to make any technique backfire is by using too many words.

6. **Do not lecture or remind when your child is ready to come out.** This is the time to provide a loving hug and move on with your day. If your child acts up again in a few minutes, just sing, "uh-oh," and repeat the technique. Some kids require more than one or two trips when they're first learning about "uh-oh." Don't sweat it. That's normal.

7. **Have fun with your kids when they're behaving.** In order for this technique to work, do you think it might be smart to have a lot of fun with your kids when they're behaving? Some kids love to go to their room because it gets them away from a nasty parent.

> **A simple trick of successful parenting is to have lots of fun with your kids when they're behaving well so they'll miss you when they go to their room.**

Be silly with your kids. Have fun. Partake in the joy. Then, when they misbehave, all the fun shuts down. You're not angry and you don't yell, but you are very boring when their behavior turns sour. Teach them that a life of misbehavior is pretty dull.

What Parents Say about the "Uh-Oh Song"

Love and Logic parents tell us that the "Uh-Oh Song" works so well they don't have to use it often. What's the best part? The joy of this tool, they often remark, is that they find themselves spending less time warning, lecturing, and reprimanding, and more time playing and having fun with their tots. Now, that's the hallmark of an effective technique.

In a wonderful handwritten letter sent to us, we learned about a child who was visiting a neighbor with his mother. Just as he began to misbehave, Mom looked down at him and sang, "uh-oh." What happened? The child immediately stopped and asked, "Where am I supposed to go?" Mom merely responded, "Thanks for stopping! You can stay with us as long as you are acting sweet."

Start with the "Uh-Oh Song" at Home

Anything that works at home first has a better chance of working outside the home later. Psychologist types call this phenomenon the "transfer effect." The learning that takes place at home tends to "transfer" to other places. We always suggest that parents get the "Uh-Oh Song" locked in at home before trying it in public. Once a child learns to go to his or her room at home—and stay there—he or she is much more likely to go to the corner in the grocery store—and stay there.

Success using a corner at a store happens only if your child has first been conditioned to listen to "uh-oh" at home. When your little sweetie is acting not so sweet in the store, you may try, "Uh-oh. This is so sad. Looks like a little corner time!" and whisk your child off to spend some time next to the canned vegetables.

Walk a small distance away from your child, where you can watch him out of the corner of your eye while giving him little or no attention.

The "Uh-Oh Song" is a powerful technique for setting limits with young children. Another fabulous tool is what we Love and Logic folks call the enforceable statement. Wouldn't it be great if your kids believed that everything you said was gold? Wouldn't it be nice if they listened to you the first time?

Turning Your Words to Gold:
The Art of Enforceable Statements

"Sit still! Be quiet! Keep your hands to yourself." What's wrong with these statements? Have you ever found yourself telling a child to do something that you can't really make him do? How long does it take a kid to start testing and to realize that he can win the battle every time? Most kids learn quickly that, short of physical restraint, we cannot *make* them be quiet. Similarly, most learn quickly that we can't *make* them sit still. And, most learn quickly that we can't *make* them keep their hands to themselves. Each time we tell our kids to do something that we really cannot make them do, we give away some of our power and a whole lot of our credibility.

What happens when a parent says to two kids fighting in the backseat of the car, "Quit fighting." If the two keep up their warfare, the parent looks powerless. Short of physically separating them, a parent cannot *make* two kids stop dueling. Insightful Love and Logic parents recognize this and avoid the trap by using enforceable statements. Simply stated, enforceable statements describe limits that we can actually enforce 100 percent of the time. Instead of saying, "Quit fighting," a Love and Logic parent says something like, "I charge two dollars a minute to listen to fighting in the car. Will you be paying me with chores, cash, or some of your toys?"

Turn Your Words into Gold:
The Art of Enforceable Statements

Unenforceable Statements	Enforceable Statements
"Hurry up! Get ready! We need to leave!"	"The car is leaving when the timer goes ding."
"Stop picking your nose! That's gross."	"I will play with you as long as your finger stays out of your nose."
"Pick up your toys!"	"Feel free to keep the toys that you pick up."
"Eat! For crying out loud, eat!"	"See the clock? When the big hand reaches the top, that means dinner is over."
"Stop shouting! You make me crazy when you yell so loud!"	"I'll listen as soon as your voice is as calm as mine."
"Brush your teeth!"	"I allow kids to have treats only when they protect their teeth by brushing."

Mornings—without Enforceable Statements

Almost every parent of a young child complains about mornings. Have you ever been amazed by how long it takes to leave the house with a young child? Many parents find themselves being late to work and torn between a boss who complains about tardiness and a child who takes forever to get ready. Charlotte was such a child. Here's how her mother used to handle the problem.

Charlotte once believed that mornings are like the art of making fine wine—never rush it. Her mom tried everything she knew. "Put your clothes on," she begged as she rushed to get herself ready. Fifteen minutes later, when she would check on Charlotte, she'd see her with one sock on, her pants half on, and her shirt unbuttoned. "Put your clothes on!" she'd repeat, six or seven times.

Finally, from sheer frustration, she'd run in and put Charlotte's clothes on her. Then she'd sit her down with a nice, hot bowl of oatmeal. Charlotte made sculptures as the cereal slowly hardened. She was really quite artistically gifted.

"Eat it, Charlotte! How many times do I have to tell you to eat your oatmeal! There are starving kids all over the world! You don't know how lucky you are to have that food! You eat it!"

About thirty minutes later, Charlotte would typically whine, "It's cold."

At the end of her parental rope, Mom would say, "It wouldn't be cold if you'd just eat it when you get it! For crying out loud. I'll heat it up for you, but this is the last time!"

Finally, as they'd be getting ready to leave, Charlotte's mom would ask, "Where's your coat?"

"I don't know," Charlotte would whimper.

"Didn't I tell you to get your coat? Where is it? Hurry up!"

Mornings—with Enforceable Statements

Thank goodness parenting does not have to be this challenging. When I met this frustrated, exhausted mother, we talked about enforceable statements and how they could help her, especially in the morning.

The first thing she learned to say is, **"Breakfast is served until six-thirty."** She showed Charlotte what six-thirty looks like on a large clock. "When the big hand gets to where this smiley face sticker is on the clock, breakfast is over."

After these two sweet and simple sentences, Mom went into another room and bit her tongue. This was one of the most challenging things she'd ever done—saying those words, only those words, and nothing more. She was accustomed to giving Charlotte lectures about starving children, eating food when it's hot, and how lucky we are to have food. But she didn't. Good job, Mom!

When six-thirty came along, she walked over to the table where Charlotte was playing with her food, picked up her plate, and said with sincere empathy, "Breakfast is over."

Charlotte immediately began to cry. "I'm going to be hungry!"

Mom bit her tongue and said nicely, "Hang in there, sweetheart." To enforce the lesson, she called Charlotte's school the day before and told her teacher that she wasn't starving her daughter, but instead was doing a little Love and Logic training session. Mom also made sure that her teacher knew Charlotte had had an opportunity to eat, but chose to miss it. And Mom said, "Please, do not give her a snack in the morning because you feel sorry for her."

Directly after removing her plate, Mom used another enforceable statement. **"Hey, sweetie. Just so you know, I allow children to have treats only when they protect**

their teeth by brushing after eating." Then she kept her mouth shut again. Good job, Mom! Smart parents don't waste their breath with unenforceable statements like, "Brush your teeth. I said brush your teeth, Charlotte. Did you hear me? I said to brush your teeth now!"

Charlotte, looking a bit surprised, asked, "What if I don't brush my teeth?"

Mom took another breath and calmly replied, "That would be sad. But try not to worry about it."

Will Charlotte be inspired to listen to her mom when she uses enforceable statements like these? Yes! Why? Because they consist of meaningful words—words that Mom can back up with actions. Finally, as Charlotte is standing in the kitchen wearing footie pajamas and bunny ear slippers, her mom tries another enforceable statement. **"The car is leaving in ten minutes."** Again, Mom bites her lip and says nothing. Great job, Mom!

When ten minutes go by and Charlotte still doesn't have her clothes on, what does Mom do? She silently scoops up the clothes, puts them in a plastic bag and picks up Charlotte. Needless to say, guess who's yelling, "I'm not ready! I'm not dressed!"?

"No problem," says Mom. "Your clothes are in this bag. Time to leave." She carries Charlotte to the car and off they go.

❤ ❤ ❤

Charlotte's mother wrote us a letter. It ended with these words: "I only had to do this once. And the daycare staff still can't believe how fast she got dressed!"

Obviously, we don't recommend using this with your fifteen-year-old, and to the best of our knowledge, it doesn't work well on spouses! But for toddlers and preschoolers, parents keep telling us about its magic. From that day on, Charlotte's mom made no more than three statements each morning:

- "Breakfast is served until six-thirty."
- "I allow kids to have treats only when they protect their teeth by brushing."
- "The car leaves at seven o'clock."

Many parents find that once they've tried enforceable statements, they never go back to their old ways. They also find this strategy for setting limits, combined with providing plenty of small choices, supercharges their effectiveness as parents. ◄»

Decreasing the Odds of Rebellion

In Chapter 1, we learned why control is such a powerful basic emotional need. We also learned that the more choices we provide over smaller issues, the more likely children—and adults—will comply when we say "no" or ask them to do something.

King George of England wasn't a Love and Logic parent. As you probably remember, he was a bit bossy with the colonists, dictating that they couldn't do this and couldn't do that and they definitely had to pay him his share of taxes. Yep, he was a major drill sergeant parent. If he drove an SUV today, he'd be the parent who yelled at Little League games, telling his kids exactly how they should hold the bat, stand, run, catch, throw, and breathe.

We all know what happened to King George with the colonies. We all know what happens to parents who try to micromanage their kids: Serious rebellion.

Is it true many people have such strong needs for freedom and control that they will eventually do anything to get these met, including putting their own lives at risk? Yes, people have some fascinating ways of sabotaging limits when they feel domineered or coerced. They...

- might fight us head on by doing the opposite of our limits.
- might fight us by "forgetting" to comply with our limits.
- might fight us by "failing to hear" our limits.

- may battle us by following one of our limits yet "accidentally" breaking another of our limits in the process.
- might wage war with us by finding many other creative ways of showing that we don't get to make the rules.

To prevent this sad state of affairs, wise parents make a habit of providing plenty of small choices over small issues—so they can decrease the odds of rebellion over big issues. In other words, they give away the control they don't want or need—so they can increase the odds of compliance over limits they absolutely do want and need. To review the effective use of choices within limits reread pages 28 and 29. For now, let's see another example.

Although his parents don't use Love and Logic, Nathan is a sweet little kid. He and Mason, both about five, were watching a movie one evening when Mason was having a sleepover. Mason's dad is a Love and Logic pro. Here's what happened as it was getting close to bedtime.

"Guys," Dad questions as he enters the room, "do you want to go to bed now or in thirty minutes?" (Of course, Dad asked this question thirty minutes before he actually wanted them get in bed. As such, he's just fine with whatever they decide.)

Mason smiles at his dad, and says, "An hour."

Nathan agrees, "Yeah, an hour. That's good."

Dad giggles, "Nice try. Let's make it thirty minutes." (If the boys had been nasty and defiant, rather than just having some goodhearted fun, he could have replied, "Let's make it now.")

Nathan's eyes dart toward Mason, who answers, "Okay...but I wish it was an hour."

Dad agrees, "Yes, wouldn't that be nice?" ◀))

Ten minutes later, Dad asks, "Do you guys want a story first, or no story?"

"A story!" both agree.

"Great. Okay!" Dad answers enthusiastically. "Do you want to hear about the turtle who didn't want to go to school, or do you want to hear about Muffin, the kitty who thinks he's a dog?"

They opt for the confused kitty.

After the brief story, Dad asks another thoughtful question: "You guys have to decide where you're going to brush your teeth. Do you want to brush them upstairs or downstairs in the utility room with that cool sink?"

As an adult, you may be thinking, "Who cares about such little choices?"

The answer to your question is, "Just about everyone."

Over the past four decades, we've learned that it isn't so much the size of the choice, but whether it is given. As parents, don't worry about the magnitude of the choices you give, concern yourself with the consistency with which you provide the small ones.

Let's get back to the boys and their bedtime. Dad continues with the silly yet powerful choices.

"Would you two like a glass of water near your bed, or do you want to come to the sink anytime you get thirsty? Do you want to sleep in bed, or do you want to pull all the covers onto the floor and pretend you're camping? Wouldn't that be cool? Well, you decide. Do you want your light on, or off?"

Mason's father is now done with the choices. Up to this point, has he made plenty of small "deposits" into their bank accounts of control? No doubt! Now, it's time for him to make a withdrawal. "Guys, it's bedroom time. I take kids to the park in the morning when I see that they have gotten enough sleep."

"No! No! We don't want to go to bed. We're not tired!"

"Hey, don't I give you lots of choices? Didn't you just decide…" and Dad runs down the list. Then, with great love in his eyes, he says, "Well, this last choice is mine. Time for bed. See you in the morning."

❤ ❤ ❤

In the morning, at bedtime, and any other moment when we have to set limits, we can up the odds of success by using few words, providing enforceable statements, and taking advantage of the control we've shared. By doing so we can take potentially frustrating times and turn them into happy ones. That's what the magic of Love and Logic is all about.

Love and Logic Experiment #5

Hassle-Free Mornings
Review Charlotte's story on page 94.

Parents all over the country comment on how frustrating it can be to get their young kids ready for daycare or school in the mornings.

Charlotte's mother used the following statements to save herself—and Charlotte—a world of grief:

- "Breakfast is served until six-thirty. This is what six-thirty looks like on the clock."
- "I give treats to kids who protect their teeth by brushing."
- "The car leaves at seven o'clock. This is what seven o'clock looks like on the clock."

Practice them over and over again in the shower.

Practice these statements over and over again in the shower, while driving to work, each night just before falling asleep, or any other time you are alone and have some time to think.

Have a Love and Logic morning with your kids.

After you've practiced and feel confident, try this approach one morning. Once again, review Charlotte's story to remind yourself of how she operated.

Remember: Actions speak louder than words. Set the limit once and follow through. For example, if your child fails to finish breakfast on time, lock in the sincere empathy, remove his or her plate, and avoid the lectures.

Call your child's daycare or school and let them know what you are doing and why. Ask them to avoid lecturing your child or rescuing him or her by providing extra snacks before lunch.

Pack a bag with an extra set of your child's clothes and place it by the door.

If your child continues to procrastinate, point at the bag and ask calmly, "Sweetie, would you like to go to school with your clothes on your body or your clothes in a bag?"

If your child still doesn't get dressed, grab the bag and head for the car. What's the good news? Most parents only have to do this once!

CHAPTER SIX

Turning Misbehavior into Wisdom

Empathy Opens the Heart and the Mind to Learning

In Chapters 4 and 5, we learned Love and Logic Rule #1:

> **Remain a healthy role model. Do this by setting limits and taking care of yourself in loving, unselfish ways.**

Rather than displaying frustration, anger, or using threats and warnings—we set enforceable limits, avoid giving repeated warnings, provide kids with a healthy sense of control, and replace too many words with meaningful actions.

An essential partner to that rule is Love and Logic Rule #2:

> **Turn every mistake or misbehavior into a learning opportunity.** ◀ッ

How can we make this second rule a reality? Provide a sincere dose of empathy *before* delivering consequences. As you'll see, this can make the difference between a child learning wisdom from a consequence and one who merely has a "meltdown" of anger, frustration, or resentment. Over the course of years, this can also make the difference between enjoying lifelong relationships with our kids or not.

Sincere empathy, provided before the "bad news," opens a child's heart and mind for learning. Anger, in contrast, creates a child who blames others for his or her mistakes. Empathy activates the portion of the brain responsible for learning and thinking. Frustration, anger, or sarcasm activates the parts responsible for survival. Very little learning happens when a child's brain is triggering fight or flight.

LOVE AND LOGIC RULE #2 FOR PARENTS:

Turn every mistake or misbehavior into a learning opportunity.

- Provide a strong dose of empathy before allowing your child to experience the consequences of their actions.
- Replace punishment with logical consequences.
- When possible, guide your child to solve his or her own problem.

Why is Sincere Empathy so Important?

Let's take a moment and imagine that two three-year-olds have committed the same serious misstep: Both have flushed their father's wallet down the toilet. The inspiration for this example comes from my own childhood, where I apparently did the same. Now my parents can laugh about it. Are you guessing that they did so back then?

Let's call the first imaginary tot, Henry, and see how his exasperated parent handles the situation:

Parent (with obvious anger): "Henry! I can't believe you did this! You get up to your room right now! You are in big trouble! Now I need to pay for getting this unplugged, so I'm taking your toys. This makes me so mad! Do you hear me? You are paying with your toys!"

Henry (screaming and throwing himself on the floor): "Hate you! Hate you!"

Let's call the second imaginary child, Hunter.

Parent (with obvious anger): "Hunter! I am so mad about this that I better calm down before we talk."

Ten minutes later...

Parent (with as much empathy as a parent can muster): "Oh, Hunter. This is so sad. What are you going to do to repay us for this?"

Hunter (very confused): "Huh?"

Parent (calmly): "The toilet is plugged, and the wallet is ruined. That costs money to fix. How will you pay us back?"

Hunter: "But I just three. Don't gots money."

Parent: "Would you like to hear what some three-year-olds do?"

Hunter: "What?"

Parent: "Some pay by selling some of their toys."

Hunter: "No!"

Parent: "Some pay by doing a lot of extra chores."

Hunter: "Uh—help Mommy and Daddy?"

Parent: "Yes."

Hunter: "Yes. I like it."

❤ ❤ ❤

Some questions about Henry and Hunter...

• Which is angrier? Which is calm enough to think and learn?
• Which is more likely to become resentful? Which is more likely to become responsible?

- Which will find it easier to blame their parent? Which will more likely blame their own poor decision?
- Which child is learning how to become angry? Which is learning how to solve problems?
- Which parent is most likely to end each day stressed and exhausted? Which parent is more likely to experience joy and fulfillment in parenting?

Did you notice how both parents expressed anger? Which expressed it in a healthier way?

Since writing the first edition of this book, we've realized that we've done a poor job of helping parents understand that it's okay— actually very healthy—to display anger from time to time. 🔊 The key is to do so without feeling compelled to administer discipline at the very same time. Notice how Hunter's parent took a brief break to take a deep breath, calm down and think. Notice also how this allowed the parent to provide loving empathy while guiding their child toward thinking and problem solving.

Again, which parent do you suppose is happier with being a parent at the end of each day? Which—very sadly—may be wondering why they ever had kids? Which ends up in more power struggles with their child? Which is more likely to enjoy a rewarding, lifelong relationship with their child?

We have to repeat it. Empathy, empathy, empathy. It's the spoonful of sweet and sincere sadness that helps the medicine of learning go down.

Consequences + Anger =
More anger and damaged relationships

Empathy + Consequences =
More learning and loving relationships

What Empathy Accomplishes
- Models, and therefore, teaches respect.
- Teaches children to be empathetic toward others.
- Allows the parts of the brain responsible for learning to function at high capacity.
- Makes it less likely that our children will blame us for the consequences of their poor decisions.
- Reduces resentment and the chances of "payback" behavior.
- Reduces our stress.
- Preserves the adult–child relationship.

By using empathy, we teach compassion and grace. Our children have the opportunity to learn that loving others while taking healthy care of themselves is a responsible way to live.

Mirror Neurons

I (Jim) had a sobering experience while first developing the Love and Logic approach in the early 1970s. During those early years, I focused primarily on teaching parents how to set effective limits, share healthy control, and hold children accountable with logical consequences. Sound good? Well—it did to us until we quickly discovered that only about half of the parents doing such things were experiencing success.

We soon discovered the answer to the problem: Those having good results were already in the habit of expressing love and empathy before providing consequences. They were naturally empathetic. Those who experienced the poorer results—resentment and rebellion—were not. From this experience, we quickly learned the power of empathy, even though we didn't completely understand why it was so powerful.

In the past few years, scientists studying the human brain have discovered that each and every one of us are born with sets of neurons that sync with the emotions of others. In other words, these neurons help us "mirror" the emotions of others.

When we're around positive people, how do we tend to feel? When someone around us is upset or anxious, what emotions do we tend to experience? When our children are angry, what do we tend to feel?

Mirror neurons are good. They allow us to connect with others. They allow us to provide empathy. Mirror neurons can also lead us astray. How so? They can lead us to respond to anger or sarcasm *with* anger or sarcasm. They can trigger frustration in our hearts when our kids are displaying frustration.

**Mirror neurons either cause us to rub off on others…
or cause others to rub off on us.
What choice will you make?**

A question all parents—and all leaders—must ask of themselves is, "Who is rubbing off on whom?" While it doesn't always come naturally, we as parents must take the lead and practice intentional empathy. When we wait to really feel it, we run the risk of allowing our children's emotions to determine ours.

I (Charles) am now very thankful for being raised with Love and Logic. As a child and teenager, I wasn't always sure. When I was about sixteen years old, some of my friends visited our home on a regular basis. Back then, I thought they did so to visit me. Now I wonder if they came to hang out with my parents.

"Your mom and dad are so cool," they'd say. "They never yell. They never nag you. They're like Mr. and Mrs. Rogers!"

Since I (Charles) am now a bit older than most readers of this book, I'd better explain the "Mr. and Mrs. Rogers" thing. Most of my generation grew up watching Mr. Rogers on television. His show personified love and innocence. He personified empathy.

How did I respond to their "Rogers" remark at the time? "Oh, you think it's so great to live around here with them. Ha! All they do is walk around and say things like, 'Oh, bummer' or 'This is so sad. What are you going to do?' I wish they'd just yell at me and get it over with."

Now that I am older, and I hope a bit wiser, I see the great wisdom in my parents' ways. The irritation I felt at the time involved the fact that empathetic people are difficult to blame. As a teen, I fantasized about them losing control. Then I'd be able to hold them responsible for my blunders. Fortunately for all of us, they'd learned this lesson early in my life. Maybe this is why I still enjoy being around them!

❤ ❤ ❤

Empathy Isn't Always Easy

A while ago, while we were presenting a Love and Logic conference, a woman piped up in the middle of our presentation and yelled, "Ain't natural!" Dazed and confused, we asked her what she meant. What was her response? "Ain't natural to be so nice to a kid when you feel like ringing her neck! What I feel like saying to my child is, 'Young'un, I brought you into this world, and I can take you right out!'"

What's the truth here? She's right—not about taking the kid out, but about the fact that empathy doesn't come naturally for most of us. Because many of us were parented with frustration and anger, empathy isn't always our immediate response. Because our mirror neurons create a sync between us and our kids, it becomes easy to automatically feel and act like our kids are feeling and acting—rather than taking the lead and remaining calm and collected. ◀》 How can we make it easier for ourselves? How can we make it feel more "natural"? Let's take a look.

Keep It Simple!

The most powerful Love and Logic parents do not get complicated with their empathy—they don't use a variety of ways to dispense it. They pick one empathetic response, one that suits them and their personality, and they stick with it. They fall back on the very same sentence—or simple sound every time they need it. Select one from below or come up with one of your own. Find one that is easy to use, feels natural, and fits your personality.

Quick Empathetic Responses
- "Uh-oh."
- "Ohhhhhh."
- "This is so sad."
- "Bummer."
- "Oh…that's never good."
- "How sad." 🔊

Why use only one? Using the same empathetic response in every situation makes learning easier for both the child and the parent. For adults as well as kids, it's easier to remember. It's that simple. The goal here is to learn one quick and easy strategy so we can deliver empathy even when we're angry, frustrated, or downright dumbfounded. Some parents we've known repeat their chosen response over and over again every night before they go to bed. Why? So it becomes a permanent and automatic part of their life. Others achieve this by writing it down on little notes and sticking them all over their house, car, and office. I visited one friend who had little yellow notes all over her house that said, "Bummer." Are you guessing this piqued the interest of more than one visitor to her home?

I (Charles) will never forget a little boy who taught me the power of using just one simple, empathetic phrase:

> He was about seven years old when he came to a Love and Logic event with his parents. Out of his earshot, his mother whispered to me, "We adopted him, and he was really out of control." 🔊
>
> I said, "But he's not now?"

And she said, "We've been using this Love and Logic stuff on him, and it's been working great."

This little guy was so cute, I couldn't resist the urge to walk over and talk to him. I noticed he had a little bandage on his knee. Have you ever noticed how young kids love to talk about their "owies"? One of the best ways to bond with little kids is to comment on their wounds. I've also noticed this working the same way with adult males. Remembering this, I asked, "Hey, wow! How did you get that boo-boo?"

The story was long and full of exciting detail. As it unfolded, I learned how he had fallen off his bike, how his mom had kissed the boo-boo, and how it still hurt just a bit. Trying to be an empathetic listener, I said, "What a bummer."

Suddenly, he stepped back and opened his eyes very wide. He looked at me and in an instant I could read his mind. It was as if he was asking, "What did I do?"

His mother, watching the whole thing, looked over at me, held in a laugh, and whispered, "Oh! We save 'bummer' for special times."

Right then and there, I realized I had accidentally mumbled this child's cue, the single empathetic response his parents had used over and over before delivering consequences.

❤ ❤ ❤

Empathy + Consequences: Kids Younger than Three

There are two main patterns for using empathy and consequences with young children, and they are both easy to learn and use. When tikes younger than age three experiment with misbehavior—throw their bottle, pull a sibling's hair, bite, spit, or kick—use the following three-step formula.

When your child misbehaves:
- Respond with empathy. Sing "Uh-oh."
- Remember the "Three L's." Change your location, the location of the problem object, or the child's location.
- Let actions speak louder than words. Don't warn, lecture, remind, or display anger.

Note: Review pages 83-91 from chapter 5.

Parents Who Use This Formula

Parents around the world have used this simple three-step formula. What have they had to say about it?

"I was always taught that I had to explain everything to my kids. What a relief it is to know they can learn from actions instead of lectures." …Ginny

"This gives me a lot more time to have fun with my kids. We just don't have all of the hassles we used to have." …Tim

"It makes for more hugging time and less crying time." …Lori

"Most of the time we don't have to take action. As soon as she hears, 'Uh-oh' she stops acting up immediately!" …Rose

Do you remember the child in chapter one? The child who waddled over to Mom's tablet, testing her "no-tablet-now" limit? Her mother sang, "Uh-oh!" *That's step one of the formula.*

Next, Mommy picked her up and gently yet firmly held her. In other words, she used one of the "Three L's." She changed her child's location. *That's step two of the formula.*

Finally, Mom remembered to let actions speak louder than words. *That's step three of the formula.*

Here's another example.

❤ ❤ ❤

Evelyn loved to be the center of attention. Many young children do. The problem was that this desire often made it next to impossible for her mother and father to have a conversation without interruptions. Mom and Dad gradually began to realize that allowing her to interrupt was not helping her develop healthy social skills—and it definitely was not helping them enjoy an emotionally close marriage.

Wise parents don't just take care of themselves in loving, unselfish ways. They also take good care of their marriage. As such, Tammy and Rubin decided to run a little Love and Logic training session. When they were both relaxed and on the same page, they started a conversation in front of their lovely Evelyn. What happened? We bet you can guess.

Rubin set a limit. "Honey, you may stay with us as long you let us talk. That means staying quiet and not pulling on our clothes."

Sweet Evelyn replied, "Okay, Daddy."

Despite her nice response, she managed to refrain from interrupting for approximately forty-five seconds.

In unison, with absolutely no anger or frustration in their voices, Tammy and Rubin sang, "Uh-oh. It looks like a little bedroom time for Evelyn." As they did, Rubin gently picked her up and placed her in her bedroom, where she was expected to stay until she was completely calm.

Did Evelyn's parents talk to her while she was in the bedroom? No. Did they stay near her room to make sure she was okay? Yes. Did they remember to avoid lecturing? Yes. Did they finish the conversation they started, so Evelyn could hear that her misbehavior didn't prevent them from visiting with each other? Absolutely. And when she finally came out, did they give her a hug and say, "We love you"? Yes! Way to go, Rubin and Tammy. ◄»

Evelyn's parents had to put some time and effort into this training session, but will this save them time later on? What are the chances that Evelyn will quickly learn that "Uh-oh" means "Let Mommy and Daddy have some time"? Are the odds higher that Evelyn will have a lot more respect for them when she becomes a teen?

Shari and Gloria are two caring moms with nine-month-old children. What words and tone of voice does each use? Which communicates lovingly high expectations? Which communicates much lower ones?

Shari's Orders

"Open up! Wider. Eat *all* of this! No! Don't spit it out! I said, no, *don't* spit. You have to eat your peas. They're *good* for you. Now don't turn your head. I said, open *up*...quit spitting! Eat your food! You are going to be hungry!"

Shari's commentary consists of *orders* or unenforceable statements. Since her child is too young to understand all of these words, he must focus on the tone of voice, facial expression, and other nonverbal cues. He sees furrowed eyebrows, a down-turned mouth, and a person who's fussing over every action. All he hears is tension. The mirror neurons in his brain are now triggered, so that he's too upset to think and learn.

By the time Shari's child understands her words, might he believe that none of them mean much except frustration? Might he be conditioned to ignore most of things she says, largely as a defense mechanism to avoid anxiety?

Bluntly put, Shari—a well-intentioned and loving mom—is training her child to believe that her orders mean nothing. She's also modeling bossy, irritable, and impatient behavior. What are the chances that she'll soon have a bossy, irritable, and impatient teen?

Now, consider Gloria, whose child is also nine months old. Notice how she uses the simple empathy plus consequence formula.

Gloria's Observations

"Whew!" she says. "Oh, you really want to spit food today. This is so sad. Looks like lunch is over." She removes the food from her child's highchair and takes him to his playpen.

When Gloria's child misbehaved, she used her empathetic response, "This is so sad." That's step one. Secondly, she took the food away from her child and changed his location. That's step two. Lastly, she let actions speak louder than words. That's step three.

What was most important here? She set limits and followed through with loving actions. No anger. No warnings. No lectures. No reminders. Are the odds high that she will enjoy a far more patient, thoughtful, and empathetic teen?

**Show your children you can handle them
without breaking a sweat.**

It's All about Love and Hope

Did you notice how each Love and Logic parent avoided anger and frustration? Did you see how they showed their kids how they can handle them without breaking a sweat? When we can do discipline this easily, we show our kids great love, and we give them hope. It's as if they begin to reason, "If my parents can handle me this easily, I must be a pretty great kid!"

With three simple steps, many parents have changed their lives and taught their tots memorable lessons. You can do it, too. For those of you who have kids over the age of three, this simple approach often continues to work well. In fact, I know a mother who used it on her teenager. How? After she caught him abusing the family car by burning rubber and driving recklessly, she locked in the empathy, changed the "location" of his set of keys, and kept her mouth shut. Although this didn't win her heaps of gratitude from him, her car stayed in one piece and the neighborhood streets were once again safe.

**Love and Logic parents look forward
to their children's misbehavior.
Why? The path to responsibility and wisdom
is paved with mistakes.**

Love and Logic Experiment #6

The Power of Empathy

*Pick just one empathetic phrase
you can use with your kids.*

Listed below are some examples used by parents across the country:

"How sad."
"What a bummer."
"This sure must hurt."
"Oh ... something like this never feels good."
"I love you. This must be hard."

Choose one of these or make up your own.

Remember to avoid sarcasm.

Sincere empathy works wonders. Sarcastic empathy results in resentment.

*Practice your single empathetic statement
over and over.*

Write the phrase over and over again on little sticky notes. Put them all over the house where you will see them throughout the day.

Say your phrase repeatedly in the shower, while you are driving, right before you fall asleep at night, etc.

Visualize or imagine yourself using this phrase with your kids. Visualize yourself staying calm and being sincere.

*Use this same response each and every time
you have to give a consequence.*

Parents often comment that this simple tool makes a world of difference with their kids. There is nothing quite like sincere empathy to build and preserve loving parent–child relationships.

CHAPTER SEVEN

Give Them the Gift of Thinking

Building Responsibility and a Healthy Sense of Self

Wouldn't it be great if, at the end of the day, your kids went to bed more tired from thinking than you? When children reach age three or so, the fun can really begin. How? When our kids misbehave or make mistakes, we can start asking them, "How are you going to solve this problem?" There is nothing more fun than watching the smoke come out of a child's ears as they think. And, there is nothing that builds responsibility and confidence faster than giving them just a bit of guidance and allowing them the satisfaction of seeing themselves be successful. Kids develop a wonderfully healthy sense of self when they see that effort and perseverance pay off. As you've surely experienced, there are few things more exciting than seeing a child overcome an obstacle and seeing their eyes light up with satisfaction.

> Families are always happier
> when parents solve their own problems—
> and their children do the same. ◄))

When a very young child starts to cry in a store because she doesn't get what she wants, it is best for a parent to use the simple "empathy plus consequences" formula. We learned this in the previous chapter. Clearly, there is no benefit in asking a one-year-old, "How are you going to solve this problem?" In contrast, with a child approximately three years or older we might experiment with handing the problem back in a loving way. What do we mean?

Come and meet little Marc and his father. As we eavesdrop on their shopping trip, we'll get a glimpse of how Love and Logic parents give the gift of thinking by guiding their children to own and solve problems.

Marc, who's almost four, often goes with his father to a drugstore. This store carries everything—including toys. Whenever they go, the toy aisle—like a black hole in space—sucks him in. He gravitates toward cars, trucks, and other objects he can pull off the shelves. Playing with them is so much fun.

Much to the chagrin of his father, we see little Marc drawn to the most forbidden toy in his household—the bow and arrow set with suction cups. His father thinks to himself, "No way! I'll have those things stuck on my forehead, on the cat, on the fine china, all over the house. No way!" Dad has some choices to make. One option might be to say something like, "Put that back on the shelf. What do you think? Do you think that money grows on trees? Besides, you're gonna put your eye out with that thing!"

Instead, his father takes a deep breath, remembers his Love and Logic training, and makes another decision. His son is old enough to do some thinking on his own. Dad waits until they stand in the long checkout line. Then he looks down at his son, smiles, and asks very sincerely, "How are you going to pay for that?" ◄»

His son whines, "What? I don't know. You're going to buy it for me!"

What is Dad's response? He whispers, "This is so sad."

Marc immediately thinks, "Oh, no. It's that 'This-is-so-sad' thing!"

Dad continues, "Would you like some ideas?"

Marc whimpers, "What?"

"Some kids decide to feel around in their pockets to see if they have some money. How would that work?"

"I don't have any money!" Marc complains.

"That's sad," Dad responds. "Would you like another idea?"

"Yes," Marc whines.

"Well," says Dad, "some kids decide to put it back on the shelf and wait until they are older and have some money. How would that work?"

Marc is unhappy and feisty. "I want it now! I want it!"

"I just have one more idea, but I'm not sure it's a good one. Some kids decide to take it out of the store and risk getting in big trouble. How would that work?"

"Oh, that's a good idea. I'm taking it!" Marc says, believing he's found the perfect solution.

Standing just behind Marc and his dad are two tough-looking guys who've been listening to the conversation and grinning all of the time. One of them turns around and says very seriously to the boy, "Yeah! Then the cops come and take you away."

Marc's eyes get really big, but he isn't ready to give in. Dad smiles down on him and says, "I'll love you no matter what happens. Good luck."

When they reach the counter, what do you suppose happens? Marc, like any other self-respecting kid, puts the bow and arrow set right on top of his father's purchases. Dad moves it off to the side, looks at the checkout lady, and says, "This cute little boy here is my son. He's going to talk to you about how he's planning to get this bow and arrow set out of the store without paying for it. I'll let you guys take care of that after I pay for my things."

In a second, without a word, Marc runs back to the toy aisle and returns the bow and arrow set to where he first grabbed it.

Walking back, he says to his father, "You would've bought it for me if you were nice." How does his father respond? With a big, loving hug, Dad whispers, "I know it's hard." As they drive away from the store, Marc is already getting over his anger. He and his father enjoy the rest of the day. As we say at the Love and Logic Institute, "Empathy soaks up emotions."

❤ ❤ ❤

Who did the most thinking here? Sweet little Marc did the lion's share. Is he now becoming better prepared for life? Did Dad prevent a power struggle? Here's the key:

• Ask plenty of sincere questions.
• Provide some suggestions.
• Set an enforceable limit.
•Avoid telling your child what to do.

**Sincere questions create thinking.
Commands create resistance.**

Guiding Kids to Own and Solve their Problems

Marc's father used five steps to help his son take ownership of the problem to solve it. The first step involves locking in the empathy "That is so sad." The second step is to ask how they plan to solve the problem. Marc's daddy inquired, "How are you going to pay for that?" When Marc responded, "I don't know," Dad moved on to step three. "Would you like some ideas?" At step four, Marc's father provided some simple suggestions. Lastly, he allowed Marc to learn from his choice rather than telling him what to do.

Marc's dad asked a lot of questions. By asking them, he accomplished a number of things. He let Marc know that the problem belonged to Marc. He sent the following message: "Son, you are capable!" He gave the neurons in his son's brain plenty of exercise. He took care of himself by allowing Marc to do most of the thinking about the problem.

**Five Steps for Guiding Kids
to Own and Solve Their Problems**
- Provide a quick dose of sincere empathy.
- Ask your child, "What are you going to do?"
- When your child says, "I don't know," ask, "Would you like to hear some ideas?"
- Offer no more than three possible solutions. After each ask, "How would that work for you?" ◀))
- Allow your child to choose—and learn from the consequences of their choice, combined with your empathy.

"How Would That Work for You?"

Marc's dad gave him some possible solutions to his problem. After each one, he asked, "How would that work for you?" That's step four. Marc was allowed to choose, and learn from his choice. Love and Logic parents actually hope for poor choices. Why? We keep saying it! The road to responsibility and wisdom is paved with mistakes. Is it best for children to make poor choices early in life, when the price tags of the consequences are low? Or is it best for them to make them later, when the price tags are very high—in possible life-or-death situations? Will Marc be happier and more responsible in the long run if he first learns about the consequences of stealing at age three, or at age twenty-three? Poor choices become far more costly with age.

"Ohhh…this is so sad. What an energy drain."

Everywhere we go, parents describe the handiness of this five-step approach. Some offer very creative and amusing applications. When children misbehave, it's not uncommon to find oneself at a loss for the type of consequence to provide. A mother we met nearly twenty years ago described how she used the five steps to provide a "generic" consequence. Apparently, her first experiment took place when her child began getting into the nasty habit of lying to her. Catching her young son shading the truth, she very theatrically declared, "What an energy drain!" Then she said, "This is so sad. When you lie, it drains my energy. How are you going to put it back?" ◀))

Dazed and confused by her display, he simply muttered, "Don't know."

Then she asked him, "Do you want some ideas?"

"Okay," was the only response he could muster.

"Well, some kids decide to clean the toilet. That puts energy back into Mom. Some kids decide to go out and clean the backyard. That puts energy back. Some kids decide to vacuum. That's an energy builder. How would one of those work for you?"

"I don't know how to do that stuff," he replied.

"Not to worry," she answered, "I'll show you how to get started. Which would you like to do?"

"Vacuum. I want to vacuum."

Telling us this story, Mom laughed as she described what he looked like as he was pushing and pulling the sweeper around the living room. Too short to easily reach the handle, he stood on his tiptoes, grabbed it, and pulled it down. As a result, the bottom of the sweeper flipped up, and he ended up vacuuming more air than carpet.

Caution!
**Wise parents never criticize their young children
when chores are not done absolutely perfectly.**

The more we criticize when they are little, the more they will resist doing chores as teens…and spouses. Instead, smart moms and dads say things like, "Wow! You worked hard. Thanks."

After vacuuming part of the living room, he looked up at her and asked, "Am I done yet? This is really hard."

In a feeble tone of voice, holding her hand up to her forehead, Mom answered, "I still feel weak…very little energy. Try some more. You're getting close."

After finishing the room, he asked again, "Am I done yet?"

Mom responded with a somewhat stronger voice, "I'm feeling much better. I bet all of the energy will be back after you finish the hall."

How did he respond? "But I'm tired."

What did she say? "I know."

Finally, just as he finished the hall, she proclaimed with great excitement, "I'm feeling much more energetic. Thank you! Give me a big hug. You did it!"

When this mother first used the "energy drain" technique, she was concerned. Why? Her son seemed to be happy afterward. Aren't kids supposed to cry and be visibly upset after being disciplined? Not necessarily. Some of the best discipline occurs when both the parent and the child feel good afterward. The parent feels good, because the child has worked hard and repaid his or her debt to society. The child feels good, because he or she experiences a sense of accomplishment and growing competence. ◄))

**Every opportunity
to own and solve a problem
enhances a child's sense
of accomplishment and confidence.**

We are always amazed at how long children can remember the lessons they learn from techniques like the "energy drain." A dad heard the story you just read. Giving it a try, he found that it worked quite well with their twins William and Audrey. When the twins started whining in the store, Mom or Dad would remark, "Oh no! Energy drain." When they left toys on the floor for Mom and Dad to trip over, Mom or Dad would sing, "Oh no! Energy drain." When they threw fits at the dinner table, these parents would chime, "Oh no. Energy drain." When the twins engaged in bouts of sibling rivalry, Mom and Dad would proclaim, "Oh no. Energy drain." As you may have guessed, little Billy and Audie became very good at doing chores to put energy back into their parents. Their mother even remarked, "I started looking forward to them acting up so I didn't have to do so much housework! I could get some extra chores done."

Before long, both children made a wise decision: "We're sick and tired of putting energy back into these parents!" What happened then? Their behavior improved. Mom joked, "That was such a bummer! Now we had less help with the chores!"

Apparently Billy and Audie had become so well behaved that their parents hadn't had a real energy drain for about two years. In the meantime, their baby sister, Lily, was born. As Lily became a toddler, she and the twins began to develop a nasty habit of arguing very loudly in the backseat of the car. Mom and Dad remembered the energy drain technique. "Oh—this arguing is really draining our energy," they remarked.

It had been over two years since William and Audrey had heard this phrase. Eyes wide, they hushed their little sister. "Stop fighting! Be quiet! Mom and Dad are gonna make us do chores!"

❤ ❤ ❤

These parents were amazed that their twins remembered the meaning of "energy drain" so long after they last heard it. They were doubly amazed by the fact that it helped to calm the sibling bickering and fighting. While every family is different, there are some general guidelines that can dramatically help diminish sibling spats.

Sibling Rivalry: Seven Suggestions

1. **Remember that some rivalry is normal.**

   When handled well by parents, it can help children learn great skills for managing life's conflicts.

2. **Experiment with providing more limits.**

   When parents set too few limits, a power vacuum develops in the home. It doesn't take long for kids to start fighting with each other to fill this position. Be sure your children know you're a strong leader.

3. **Avoid comparing your children with each other.**

   This is always sure to create great strife.

4. **In most cases, avoid trying to provide consequences for the one who "started it."**

   In most cases, it's impossible to truly know who instigated the conflict. Usually both are playing a role.

5. **Avoid trying to solve the problem for them.**

   The more we try to solve their problem, the more they will need us to solve their problem. We can't "fix" things between others, but we can guide them to own and solve the problem.

6. **Have an "energy drain" when their strife causes problems for you.**

   We typically do not recommend providing consequences for children when they are unhappy with each other. We do encourage providing consequences when this unhappiness overflows and creates headaches for their parents.

7. **Protect them from each other only when necessary.**

   When we overprotect, we create kids who believe they can battle with each other and simply rely on someone else to fix the problem. We also teach them the best way to gain our attention is by having problems with each other. Step in only when life and limb are in danger, or one child is truly victimizing another. ◀))

Again, Audrey and William's parents were amazed that their twins could remember the meaning of the "energy drain" after so much time had passed. It was proof to them that young children can learn and remember a lot more than we often believe they can. They were also surprised by how this simple tool lowered their daily worry and stress levels.

"We used to worry that we wouldn't know what to do when our kids acted up. This trick works in so many different situations that we rarely find ourselves wondering, 'Oh great. What do we do now?'"

When Your Kids Refuse to Replace Energy

The energy drain is a wonderfully powerful and flexible tool. But what's a parent to do if their child becomes so resistant that he/she refuses to put energy back? That's when many parents find themselves at a loss for what to do. All of us have been there. All of us have found ourselves wondering, "Oh, great. Now what do I do?" Love and Logic teaches a fun and effective way of handling such situations. Let's take a look at a mother who tried it out.

Little Jackson had created quite the energy drain by refusing to stay in his room after bedtime. The following morning, his parents calmly said, "Jackson, this is so sad. You really drained our energy by coming out of your room after bedroom time. How are you going to put that energy back into us?

Jack is not your run-of-the-mill tyke. Nope, he's a super strong-willed, turbocharged tot. "No! I'm not doing it. You guys are buttheads!"

❤ ❤ ❤

Delaying Consequences Gives Us Time

Oh boy! Are you guessing that Mom and Dad are somewhat perturbed? Are you guessing they are ready to provide a loving and sincere dose of empathy? We think not.

Here's the dilemma: Many of us have heard from "experts" that parents need to provide an immediate consequence when a child has an outburst like this. In reality, how many of us are really good at coming up with perfectly logical consequences, delivered with empathy, when we are upset and in the middle of driving, shopping, talking on the telephone, etc.?

Let's get real. No matter how many parenting skills we have, it's almost impossible for most of us to provide sincere empathy and appropriate consequences when we're feeling angry, overwhelmed, exhausted, or perplexed. Give yourself a break. What does this really look like? Let's take a look at how Mom and Dad dealt with little Jackson's serious defiance—and his new vocabulary word.

Hearing "You guys are buttheads" does not fill parents with joy. In fact, Jackson's parents were beginning to fantasize about behavior management techniques other than Love and Logic—illegal ones. Then they remembered:

**When you don't know what to do—
or you're too angry to think straight—
delay the consequence.**

What did they do? What does the delayed consequence sound like? Dad replied with steady sternness: "That is not okay! I'm going to have to do something about that—but not now. I make better decisions when I'm calm. Your mom and I will talk."

Is it okay to put some steel into your voice and let your kids know you are angry? Yes. In fact, it's healthy for our kids to know this from time to time. It's also healthy for us to be honest about our emotions. Notice, however, how Dad remained in control and didn't make any threats he and Mom could not back up. Notice also how he modeled something very healthy: Responsible people calm down before they act.

Jack became very quiet for about five seconds. Then he asked, "What are you gonna do?"

"We don't know yet," Mom and Dad answered. "We need to talk and give it some thought. Try not to worry."

Now Jackson was worried. "Tell me. You gotta tell me. What are you gonna do?"

Dad answered calmly, "We'll do something. Try not to worry so much."

The next morning, Jackson was up early, anticipating his playdate with Jacob, his best friend. Mom and Dad broke the sad news, "Ohhh—no. This is such a sad deal. Jackson, we just don't have the energy to drive you over to Jacob's."

Jack was shocked. "What? What! Why are you so tired?"

Mom replied, "Yesterday, when we asked you to put energy back into us, what did you call us?"

Taking a cue from some politicians, Jake replied, "I don't remember."

Patting him gently on the back, Dad added, "Oh, that bad word you called us—and then you refused to put some energy back into us for coming out of your room the night before."

"Yeah, but—I'll be good. I promise," Jack replied.

Mom and Dad countered with more empathy, "We know. This really is so sad. The good news is that we can try again some other day. Today we're staying home."

How did Jackson react? With all the fury of an exceptionally stubborn four-year-old, he hit the floor with a full-fledged temper tantrum. Mom and Dad glanced down at him and replied, "This is so disappointing. Your last fit was so much better. We're worried that you might be losing your touch. You'd better keep practicing!" What happens when we tell a strong-willed child to have a better fit?

As you can see from this example, when children refuse to replace the energy they've drained, one option is to take time to rest—instead of doing things they really want you to do. We've known parents who rested on the couch instead. ◄))

❤ ❤ ❤

What Does an Appropriate Consequence Look Like?

Delaying the consequence gave Jackson's mom and dad plenty of time to think. That's the true benefit of this technique. What did they need to consider before taking action? How can we design a consequence that teaches Jackson something about the real world? How can we design a consequence that won't seem arbitrary or designed to "get even"? How can we be sure to lock in the empathy first and remain calm? How can we design a consequence that we can actually enforce?

Appropriate Consequences:
• Fit the misbehavior.
• Focus on poor choices, not "bad" children.
• Address the present, not the past.
• Are wrapped in a loving blanket of empathy.
• Are not accompanied by lectures, reminders, or guilt trips.
• Can be enforced consistently.
•Teach your child wisdom.

Parents we meet boast about how well the delayed consequence technique works for them. They no longer have to fear not knowing what to do. They can take some time and get help from others. The best part is there are only three steps, and they're easy to remember.

First, when you don't know what to do, delay the consequence. Say, "I'm going to have to do something about this, but not now." You may decide to add, "I make better decisions when I'm calm."

Second, put together a plan. Often it helps to call a friend, talk with your spouse, or get some ideas from someone else.

Third, apply the empathy plus consequence formula.

Three Steps in Delaying Consequences
- Say, "I'll have to do something about this, but not now."
- Develop a plan that fits the misbehavior. Make sure the consequence is appropriate.
- Apply sincere empathy before providing the consequence.

One of our favorite situations happened at a Love and Logic parenting conference. It's an example of how the delayed consequence technique turned a chaotic home into a calm one.

> On the first night of our Love and Logic parenting seminar, this couple had all of the typical signs of weary parents—the mother had dark circles under her eyes, and the father had an uncontrollable twitch. They kept leaving and returning to the session…in and out, in and out, in and out. Finally, they gathered their things and left early.
>
> When they returned the next evening, they looked a little more relaxed. When conference participants were asked if anyone had experimented with Love and Logic, this father stood up and smiled a happy "yes."
>
> When asked what happened, he said, "We have six-year-old twins." The audience immediately groaned their

sympathy. "They've worn out almost every baby-sitter in town," he continued. "I'm sure you saw us coming and going yesterday. Well, they were acting so badly in the childcare you provided that we kept getting texts to come to talk to them. Finally, they acted up so badly that the lady who's running it kicked them out. She told us they couldn't come back!"

Imagine this: You are a parent. Your kids are out of control. You go to a parenting class in the hope of learning how to control them—and they get you kicked out! Feeling bad for the father, we expressed our empathy.

"Oh, it's okay," he said. "We got in the car last night and did the delayed consequence thing." You could hear the other couples' interest pique as he went on.

"When we got in the car, I looked at them in the rearview mirror and said, "Ooooooh. This is sad. Fighting like that? We're going to have to do something about it—but not now, because we're driving. We'll come up with something really good. We'll call Grandma, Grandpa, check with the neighbors. We'll figure something out. Try not to worry."

Did this dad follow step one perfectly? Absolutely!

The next day, these parents proceeded with step two. They called some friends and family, put together their plan, and covered all their bases.

The next afternoon, as they were preparing to return for the second evening of our conference, their twins asked, "Where are you going?"

"We're going to our parenting class," their mother said.

"Yeah," said their father. "We had a good time there."

The twins looked at each other and one of them protested. "You can't go!"

The other twin jumped in. "We got kicked out. You have to stay with us!"

At that moment, the doorbell rang. Who entered? A special boring babysitter selected just for this occasion.

"This is Mabel," said Dad. "She's going to watch you tonight."

"What?!" the twins echoed in perfect harmony.

"She charges ten dollars an hour if you're sweet," said their mom, "and twenty an hour if you're not…"

"…And," their father chimed in, "she's going to ask how you plan to pay her."

"What!? Please, Dad! Don't leave us here!"

Their parents wished Mabel a good night and walked out the door. They returned that night after the kids were asleep. Mabel reported that the girls had behaved rather well, and she laughed, "They kept saying, 'We don't have any money,' and they kept begging me to waive my fee!"

The next morning these parents awoke to find two very concerned kids. "We can't pay Mabel," one whined.

The other interjected, "Yeah, we told her we couldn't pay her."

How did Mom and Dad respond to this? "No problem. We'll pay her."

"Great! Cool!" replied the twins.

"But this is so sad," Dad continued. "Then you can pay us back with toys."

"Oh, good! We can do that!" said the twins.

Mom and Dad were a bit confused by this chipper response.

The twins ran into their bedroom and came back with some of their oldest, most broken toys.

Their father applied empathy. "Oooooh, bummer!" he said. "Those toys are too broken."

The twins returned to their bedroom and came back with some small plastic toys they had received at a fast-food restaurant.

"Ooooooh, bummer!" their mother said. "Those are too small."

As they described the scenario to the rest of our class, Mom and Dad giggled. "We had a blast watching them run back and forth from their rooms, desperately trying to find something they didn't like—but we'd take for payment. After several trips, the two children finally returned, very slowly, with their final pick—their favorite dolls—complete with the matching pink plastic sports car.

Dad proudly described how powerful this method was: "They came to us sniffling. Then they asked, 'Mommy— Daddy? If you spank us, can we keep our dolls?'"

❤ ❤ ❤

Dad continued, "I just said, 'no,' we used to do that stuff, but we found something better."

Mom added, "Now we realize why spanking them never worked. When we did it, they were off the hook. They could be mad at us rather than really having to think about the consequences of their actions."

The class applauded these parents for experimenting with some new ideas. We had all made a great discovery—that empathy opens kids' minds to learning, and we can plan something just right if we give ourselves permission to briefly delay consequences.

Love and Logic Experiment #7

Have an Energy Drain
The next time your child creates a problem for you, have an "energy drain."

The "energy drain" technique essentially amounts to what we call a "generic consequence." What does this mean? Simply put, parents can use this technique any time their kids create some sort of hassle for them.

Listed below are some possible reasons for having an energy drain:

- Your child lied to you about something.
- Your kids are fighting around you and it hassles your eyes and ears.
- Your child interrupts you while you are on the phone.
- Your child misbehaves at school, and you get a call from the teacher.
- Your child keeps whining and won't stop.
- Your child causes a problem for you in any other way.

The number of uses for energy drain boggles the mind.

Review "Ohhh…this is so sad.
What an energy drain" on page 123-128.

Notice how these two parents applied this technique to two different problems. One used it with lying. The other used it with sibling bickering.

Ask your child how he or she plans to recharge you.

Try saying something like this: "What an energy drain. When you interrupt me on the phone, it really tires me out. How are you planning to put this energy back into me?"

When your child says something like, "I don't know," give him or her some possible options. Extra chores are a great recharging strategy.

CHAPTER EIGHT

Don't Wait Until
They're Teenagers!

Good News about the "Terrible Twos"

Everyone has heard of the "terrible twos." It's a phrase that wreaks havoc in the hearts of parents with infants and little sweeties who are starting to crawl. They wait for their children to turn two with the same expectations as a convicted criminal awaiting a death sentence.

Two-year-olds have unjustly gotten a bad name. Sure, the second year of life is all about becoming independent and testing authority, and this can be pretty trying for parents. Are you ready for the good news?

First, experimentation with independence and testing of authority are normal and healthy signs. It's what kids at that age are supposed to do. Second, Love and Logic offers some practical tools for making this age more fun for parents. That's right—fun! Third, the lessons learned at this age pave the way for how children will deal with authority figures for the rest of their lives. In other words, the lessons we teach our kids at an early age tend to stick.

That's why Love and Logic parents don't wait fourteen years. They start when their kids are young enough to carry, so they can enjoy the teen years with kids who are respectful, responsible, and fun to be around.

> **The best predictor of
> a sweet and responsible teen
> is a two-year-old who's learned
> that your "no" means "no."**
>
> **The best predictor of
> an out-of-control teenager
> is a two-year-old who
> runs the house.** ◄))

Good News for Parents of Two-Year-Olds
- Your child's desire to be independent and to test authority is normal and healthy.
- Practical Love and Logic tools can make this age more fun for parents.
- If you parent really well during the first three years of life, chances are your child will become a responsible teenager who is fun to be around.

Becoming a Loving Authority Figure

Children thrive when they view their parents as loving and a bit strict at the very same time. The term "loving" means that the parent is warm, nurturing, positive, and empathetic. Our use of the word "strict" doesn't imply being dictatorial, mean, or punitive. It means providing firm limits and enforcing reasonably high expectations.

In essence, this combination personifies what we mean by "loving authority figure." When children lack such adults in their lives they often feel out of control and act that way. Their confidence and understanding of cause and effect suffers, so they tend to spend their lives underachieving or making poor decisions. Fortunately, it's never too early to establish yourself as a loving authority figure in your child's life. How?

Everything we've talked about thus far has been devoted to helping you achieve this goal. The four principles of Love and Logic, the two basic rules, and what we've learned about needs and wants—all of it helps parents and other care providers achieve this all-important goal.

Handle Them without Breaking a Sweat

We've said it before. The first step is showing your kids that you can handle them without breaking a sweat. In other words, show them you can handle their misbehavior without frustration, anger, threats, or repeated warnings.

One of our favorite examples is what happened with little Arturo. Have you ever noticed how two-year-olds tend to pick restaurants as the best places for all-out free-for-alls? Because this had become somewhat of a chronic problem with little Artie, his mother and father decided to try a bit of Love and Logic. After spending some time planning, Mom and Dad decided to have an "Authority Figure Training Session" (AFTS) at a local restaurant.

Wise parents plan ahead. They predict when their kids will have fits and put a plan together before they go. Then, they can actually look forward to their children misbehaving. The reason? The road to wisdom is paved with mistakes.

When Artie and his family went out to eat, he refused to sit in his highchair, and started to whine, "I hate this place! I hate this place! No!"

His father looked at him with sadness in his eyes and asked softly, "Is this a wise decision, Art?" Arturo continued his fit.

Arturo's mom piped up sweetly, "How sad. Looks like Artie needs to go and sit in the back room until he understands how to behave when he's eating with us." Earlier in the week, these Love and Logic parents had phoned a number of restaurants until they'd found one whose manager agreed to help them out with a little "thinking area" for Arturo. (By the way, some parents simply use the restroom as the "thinking area." Others gently buckle their child into a stroller and roll them outside by the entrance. They roll the stroller up to a boring wall and wait with the child until he or she is calm.)

Artie began to wail as his father carried him back to the coatroom of the restaurant. Luckily, Artie's dad knows a neat trick for handling wailing and other such frustrating behavior.

> ***One way to stop irritating behaviors is to encourage them.***

Encourage an obnoxious behavior? Why? When we encourage a child to do something he's going to do anyway, we remain in charge. We avoid a power struggle. Encouraging the behavior also causes many children to reason, "My parents actually want me to throw this fit! I'll show them. I'll stop. Nobody can make me throw a fit if I don't want to."

Arturo's father looked into his eyes and calmly said, "The really good thing about this room is that it's okay to cry and yell back here. Sometimes it's just best to scream it out. I think it would be good if you just yelled as loud as you can."

Artie glared back at his father. "No! I don't want to yell!"

Dad responded, "Okay, but I think it might help."

Art sat for about two seconds, then stood up and began to stomp loudly. His father said softly, "Make sure you do some good stomping if you're going to stomp. The last time you stomped it was really boring. I'll wait right over here until you are ready to act nice. Then you can come out."

Children cannot achieve true autonomy without first learning how to respond properly to authority. ◀))

Kids cannot become truly responsible, happy, and independent until they've learned how to deal with authority in an appropriate way. Real freedom cannot be attained without accepting and sharing respect and responsibility.

Age two, Arturo's father learned, is all about teaching kids how to take "no" for an answer. He also learned some Love and Logic magic to make this happen. Since he and his wife had locked in the "Uh-Oh Song" at home, Artie only had to spend a few minutes in the back room.

Wise parents know that the first step toward getting their toddlers to behave in public is getting them to behave at home.

A much cuter and sweeter Arturo walked back to the table with his dad. What did his parents say when he returned? They didn't lecture, threaten, or rub salt into the wounds. Instead, they said enthusiastically, "Good to have you back, sweetie! We love you." They resisted the urge to say something like, "I hope you learned your lesson, young man." They know that the consequence is the lesson and their son is smart enough to learn from it.

A while ago, we met a single mother with two little boys and one little girl. She used a different strategy for dealing with restaurant rampages. Susie was having a very bad evening, so bad that she began spreading mashed potatoes in her hair and wailing, "Yucky 'tatoes! Yucky 'tatoes."

Mom picked up her cell phone, dialed a number, and said, "It's time!" Ten minutes later, her friend arrived at the restaurant, carried Susie to the car, and took her home. When Mom walked in the door with the boys, she made sure that each was eating an ice cream cone.

Little Susie wailed, "Ice cream! They got ice cream? Not fair!"

Mom turned to her and said softly, "What a bummer. This is so sad. I give ice cream to children who act sweet when we're in a restaurant. By the way, which toy are you going to use to pay for your babysitting?"

❤ ❤ ❤

Do you think Susie is beginning to see her mommy in a new light? Is Mom establishing herself as a loving authority figure? Are you guessing Susie will be quite a bit sweeter the next time they eat out?

More Thoughts on What We Mean by "Loving Authority Figure"

As we now know, there's one cardinal rule for the first few months of a child's life: Do everything to meet your infant's basic needs. Snuggle, make massive amounts of eye contact, smile, and do your best to relieve any physical or emotional pain or discomfort. When an infant cries, we do not leave him or her alone in his room or crib. Instead, we meet the needs that are causing the crying.

While loving parental authority figures want their children to be happy, and they meet their children's basic needs as consistently as possible, they don't become "doormats." They don't respond to "wants" in the same way they respond to needs. If they did, they'd be run ragged by a demanding and obnoxious toddler. They know that the first rule of parenting is to remain a good role model by taking good care of themselves. They also realize how important it is that they teach their children the difference between needs and wants.

People almost universally remark that "strict, but loving" parents, teachers, coaches, religious leaders, and other adults

were the people who had the greatest positive influence on them when they were kids.

Love and Logic believes in this combination and teaches us how to become the most loving people in our children's lives while at the same time being some of the most powerful.

What Love and Logic Authority Figures Give Kids
- Unconditional love and respect
- High expectations and firm limits
- Some freedom within those limits
- Time and encouragement to struggle through difficult challenges
- Guidance in solving problems within those challenges
- An understanding of the difference between needs and wants
- Positive, confident role models

True Authority Figures Are Both Powerful and Kind

Truly successful authority figures don't have a long list of rules to be followed. They enjoy respect, because they offer it. They set limits, because they understand that we all need them.

They give children choices, because they know that decision making prepares a child for a world filled with important, potentially life-and-death choices. As a result, children fed on a diet of Love and Logic develop a healthy, confident, internally motivated sense of self that believes, "Yes! I can do it! Yes! I'm capable!"

> **Wise parents begin the process of becoming loving authority figures during the first days of their child's life.**

Through eye contact, smiles, hugs, and meeting basic needs, parents lay a foundation of love. As "wants" begin to emerge for their child, they begin to set very firm, yet kind, limits. They realize the best way to have fun with their teenagers is to be strong and loving with their toddlers.

They also know that young children learn some of their first lessons about loving authority while playing with their parents. When it comes to little kids, play equals learning.

> Four-year-old Xavier loves to wrestle with his mom and dad and play roughly. His mother and father wrestle with Xavier because they know he enjoys it, but they are careful to make sure that nobody gets hurt. Xavier pushes against his father or mother, who pushes back with some gentle intensity, holding Xavier in place. Then he or she quickly lets go, surprising the little guy a bit.
>
> "More! More!" Xavier yells, giggling, when his parent lets go. Then Xavier's mom or dad holds him gently, and Xavier shouts, "Let me go! Let me go!"
>
> His parent lets go. Then, in a surprise attack, he gently jumps on top of Xavier, until Xavier squeals with delight, "Get off me!" His parent holds on a few seconds longer, then lets him go. All of them have a great time.

❤ ❤ ❤

This type of wrestling play may be more common with little boys than little girls, but it's good for girls, too. What can kids learn from this? They learn that their parents love them. They learn that sometimes their parents allow them to have some control. They learn that their parents are more than able to overpower them—but their parents are careful not to be hurtful. All told, they learn that their parents are loving and powerful at the same time.

What Kids Learn from Wrestling Play
- Their parents love them.
- Their parents are strong people and can control them.
- Their parents won't control them unless it's necessary.

- Parents are people who are powerful, kind, and gentle at the same time.
- They love their parents and want to be like them. ◄))

A little gentle "roughhousing" helps kids bond with their parents and teaches them about authority. If you've ever had the opportunity to watch documentaries about how wolves live in the wild, you know they have a rather complex social order. The way they learn to live with the pack and be productive members of their community is to wrestle with their parents when they're pups. Now—let's be clear. We don't place children on the same level as animals, even though they can act like wild wolves from time to time.

Once in a while, the father or mother wolf will put a large paw right on top of the little pup and growl a bit. The little pup will look up and think, "Uh-oh!" and then the parent will let the pup up quickly. No one gets hurt, but the young wolves begin to understand that they can have fun and declare their independence, but they aren't in charge of the pack. Is it good for kids to believe they run the show, or is it healthy for them to see their parents running it?

Love and Respect: Two Parts of a Whole

The most effective parents understand that power and kindness must remain counterparts. As such, our "big picture" goal is to parent in such a way that our children fall in love with us and respect us. When this happens, the odds are very high that they will internalize our values.

When this internalization happens, part of us lives in their hearts, guiding them in all they do. As they grow and mature, therefore, they come to rely on the kind yet powerful values residing in their hearts—rather than needing constant micromanagement.

Great parenting is great leadership. Effective leaders understand that their primary job is to inspire their followers toward a shared vision. They also understand that they can't be effective leading from behind. Constantly prodding and pushing people toward the goal leads to plenty of perspiration, but little or no inspiration. Great parents—like great leaders—walk ahead. They mostly rely on their enthusiasm, modeling, and their ability to help their children see for themselves why it's more rewarding to make good choices rather than poor ones.

> **Great leaders establish compassionate authority**
> **while sharing the control they don't need or want.**
> **Love and Logic parents do the same! ◀»**

Kids Don't Come with Instruction Manuals

None of our kids were born with an instruction manual tied to one of their toes. We're guessing that none of yours were either. Because of this, we all struggle and fall short of the ideal. Making matters even more challenging, many of us realize that our own parents sit on our shoulders—so to speak—nagging us about how to parent. These subconscious messages, developed from our own experiences as children, often become the messages that direct how we act toward our children. If we were treated with great love and respect, we find it easier to provide it for our kids. If we weren't, we often find ourselves vacillating between acting just like our parents and trying to compensate by behaving like their opposite.

There have been many times during both of our lives when we wished we'd handled things with our kids by being more consistently loving, more patient, or more assertive. Fortunately, it doesn't require perfection to raise great kids. As long as we are constantly striving toward a healthy balance of love and logic, the chances of success are good. Occasional mistakes with being a bit too permissive or a bit too strict aren't going to damage our kids.

Sadly, some parents never successfully establish themselves as loving authority figures—healthy leaders in the home—because they don't find balance between providing love and expecting respect. Some believe that love and respect are achieved by becoming a permissive doormat who always rescues the kids. Others believe the best route involves trying to control every movement their children make. Still others alternate between these two extremes, never quite finding middle ground.

Parents Who Are Dictators

Sometimes we are raised with messages in our minds that guide us to "bark" orders rather than set limits in loving ways. At the Love and Logic Institute, we refer to these parents as "Drill Sergeants." If their children don't follow their commands with precision, these parents wield lectures, threats, and punishments in an attempt to assert control. Isn't it ironic that parents who attempt to hoard control wind up losing most of it?

The environment such parents create is much like a dictatorship. Under dictatorial rule, people don't learn to make decisions. Rather, they learn to do what they're told only to avoid punishment or to earn rewards. Children raised by drill sergeants don't learn to think for themselves simply because they are rarely allowed to. They also fail to learn from their poor decisions, because they become more focused on the parent's anger than the natural and logical consequences. When children are reprimanded or punished with anger or frustration, they experience anxiety, fear, or anger. These feelings have a profound impact on brain chemistry. Portions of the cortex devoted to learning cause and effect are inhibited, while portions devoted to fight or flight are stimulated. As such, children of drill sergeants become far more adept at hiding bad decisions or defending them than learning to make more responsible ones.

This explains why we often see two types of teens created by drill sergeant parents. Some teens openly rebel or sneak around behind their parents' backs. These teenagers make lots of poor choices, just to show their parents who's boss. Other teens with drill sergeant parents remain compliant and passive…but they never learn to say "no" to others. Faced with peer pressure, they quickly follow the flock.

"Drill Sergeant" Parents
- Bark orders that they demand to be followed.
- Discipline with anger and frustration.
- Make it difficult for their children to learn from mistakes.
- Inspire fear and resentment rather than problem solving.
- Create teenagers who can't think for themselves. ◀》

The following family story is a sobering example of what can happen to kids brought up by drill sergeant parents. Not all of our stories have such tragic results, but we were moved by this story and believe it makes a memorable point.

A father we met at a conference felt embarrassed in front of teachers and other parents because he'd made so many mistakes. Apparently, he was raised in a family where everyone was bossed around by a rather authoritarian father.

Never learning anything different, he accepted this way of parenting as the only way. Also believing that it worked when he was a child, he followed suit with his own kids. Now he was coming to a Love and Logic conference with hopes of encouraging others to avoid his mistake.

A Tale of Two Teens

Joseph had two children who were as different as day and night. When the first was born, one of the nurses in the maternity ward looked at this baby girl and exclaimed, "Oh, what a sweet child! Oh, how I wish I could take her home."

"That nurse was right," Joseph told us. "From the beginning, Jesse always tried to figure out what we wanted, so she could please us. We told her what to do, and she did it."

Joseph continued, "Our second child soon came along. The head maternity nurse looked at her and didn't say a thing. She was probably thinking, 'What a sweet little girl. She's going to give them a run for their money!'"

Maternity nurses and others working with very young families often develop an uncanny ability to see into a child's basic temperament or personality. Why? Because they see so many newborns. Joseph's second little baby, Jacqueline, turned out to be a real challenge. She wouldn't eat when she was supposed to eat, she cried much of the time, and she soon became a rebellious child.

"As she grew up," he added, "she tried to find out exactly what we wanted—so she could do the opposite. We raised them the same, but they turned out so different!

"Jesse, the older one, came to breakfast one morning wearing a skirt that was far too short. When I demanded that she change into something more appropriate, she sulked a bit—but ended up wearing a dress akin to those worn by prairie women in the old frontier days. Like I said, she aimed to please.

"Jacqueline, the youngest, also tried to wear that short skirt. When I demanded that she change, she wore a long dress to school, left the short skirt on underneath, and ditched the dress once she arrived at school.

"Jesse always did what she was asked," Joseph told us, "and Jackie always fought back. We brought them up the same," he repeated. Then he became very, very quiet before telling the rest of his story. "The girls took the keys to the car one night, without permission. The high school kids in town had gotten into the habit of drag racing on a strip of road just outside of town. That was the last time I saw them alive. I'm here today, not to collect your sympathy, but because I don't want you to lose your kids the way I lost mine.

"Jackie was strong-willed, and it's obvious that I lost her by bossing her around. She rebelled by making bad decisions, just to prove she could have her own way. But I lost Jesse by bossing, too. When her sister invited her to go racing, she didn't know enough to say, 'I better not. This is not a wise decision.' We never taught her to think for herself. We just told her what to do and how to do it. We turned her into a perfect target for some of her rebellious peers. If it hadn't been her sister, it probably would have been someone else."

❤ ❤ ❤

As much as we don't like to hear what happened to Joseph, we still tell his story. Why? Because it helps all of us recognize the dangers of the drill sergeant approach.

Parents Who Search and Rescue

At the other end of the spectrum are parents who try to make their kids happy all of the time. They perform like helicopters, constantly hovering and rescuing their children from the consequences of their poor decisions and irresponsible behavior. What's the unfortunate result? They raise children who soon believe that the world revolves around them and they should never be held accountable.

Sitting at the dinner table, Eric is served some eggs by his mother. Upon seeing them, he says, "Yuck! I don't want that! No!"

His mom says, "Honey, I made them for you. You need to eat your eggs."

"No!" the boy insists. "I'm not eating them! I hate them!"

"Oh, honey," his mother says, "all right. What do you want?"

"I want Pop Tarts!" the child demands.

"Okay, sweetie," his mother says, "I'll make you Pop Tarts this time, but not again. Drink your orange juice."

"I don't want orange juice," he whines angrily. "I don't want it! I want soda!"

"Honey, soda isn't for breakfast. That's not what we have..."

"I want soda!" he yells.

"Okay, just this time. But only this time, okay?"

❤ ❤ ❤

This mother, trying to be a good mom, provided a full-service cafeteria menu every morning. Whenever he refused to eat what she served, he got what he demanded. Trying to be strict on occasion, Eric's mom would say, "No. You're eating that. I'm not getting you anything else." Eric would refuse to eat and wait it out.

Two hours later, after not eating, he'd come to his mother and whine, "I'm hungry." Guess what would happen? She'd invariably rush to prepare him another menu item.

When Eric turned seven, he developed the habit of forgetting his lunch. Calling his mother from school, he'd demand that she be more responsive to his needs. Soon she'd arrive at the door, carrying two sack lunches. Why two? Just in case he lost another before lunch.

When Eric was twelve, his teacher assigned a science project. He complained to his mother, "But this is really hard. Not fair."

"Don't worry," she replied, "I'll take care of it." Then she completed it for him. She even earned an "A."

When Eric was seventeen, Mom hired the best lawyer in town to extricate him from some hot water involving a girl and plenty of beer; when he was twenty-three, Eric was discovered stealing jewelry his mother had inherited from her grandmother; as an adult, Eric moves from woman to woman conning each for as long as he can. Who knows how many grandchildren his mother now has.

❤ ❤ ❤

Isn't that ironic? You treat kids well—you do everything for them—and they end up treating *you* badly! Why? Because when we continually rescue our kids, they become dependent on us, which eventually fills them with resentment. This syndrome is called "hostile dependency." When kids are forced to be dependent on someone, they become resentful, because down deep, every human being yearns to be free, competent, and independent. Down deep, Eric knows his mother crippled him. Now he hates her for it but ironically looks for the same treatment from every young woman he meets.

The more we rescue our kids from their poor decisions and life's manageable struggles, the more they will resent us in the long term. ◀)

When Eric's mother asked, "How could you do that—steal jewelry—after all we've done for you?" Eric said, "You never did anything for me. You never cared."

The good news is that it's never too late to change. Yes! An old dog *can* learn new tricks. Why are we so sure? Because of the many parents we've met who've changed their ways. I (Charles) received a letter from a father who saw himself as a "recovering helicopter dad." In his letter, he described how he used to park his car across the street from his son's school, sit there, and focus his binoculars on the playground. When his child went out for recess, he'd keep watch just to make sure that nothing bad happened. After learning Love and Logic, Dad realized how he was crippling his son. Now he allows his son to learn from the occasional playground disputes that every child encounters. Yes! It's never too late to change.

Helicopter Parents
- Continually hover over and "save" their children.
- Try too hard to make their children's lives "perfect."
- Create feelings of "hostile dependency" in their kids.

- Bring up children who don't know how to be responsible.
- Cause kids to feel unhappy and incapable.

Both drill sergeant and helicopter parents love their kids and do what they do because they believe it's right. Unfortunately, none of these parents successfully establish themselves as loving authority figures. Neither the drill sergeant nor the helicopter parent is able to be strict and loving at the same time. Neither provides love while simultaneously inspiring respect. Neither prepares his/her children to make wise choices in a sometimes confusing and dangerous world.

Without speaking a word, both say to their kids, "Sweetie, you are so incapable that I have to think for you. I have to constantly save you from yourself."

Why Do We Parent the Way We Do?

Obviously, how we were treated as kids has a great impact on how we parent. Our tendency is to move in one of two ways. Those of us who believe that the parenting we received was great—made us who we are today—will usually gravitate toward that style. In contrast, those of us who experienced pain as children will often move in a very different direction—sometimes to the opposite extreme. Sometimes we are aware of these decisions on a conscious level. More frequently, we've made this decision on a much deeper, subconscious level.

One of the primary goals of Love and Logic is to help parents make conscious, effective choices about how to parent based on solid research…rather than unconscious choices based on incomplete information, myths, or past hurts. To do so, let's take a look at some common themes.

- **"I don't want my kids to have to struggle like I did."** Anita grew up in a loving home, but money was always tight. The family used crates for chairs, started a garden, and raised chickens for food. She grew up feeling that she would make things different for her own kids. She struggled and eventually developed a successful business. With her own children, she spends most of her time giving them everything they want and keeping them happy. She can't understand why they're so demanding and ungrateful.

- **"I hate my parents for what they did to me."** Rob grew up with parents who yelled and screamed. Never knowing when he might be ridiculed or hit, he had a painful childhood. When he looked down at his newborn daughter, Emily, he whispered to her, "You will never feel the pain I did!" Like Anita, he spends his life protecting his child from the world. ◀))

  Both Anita and Rob are reacting to past hurts. While their motivations are pure, both of them run the risk of raising children who are entitled, demanding, and unable to make responsible choices. Children need to struggle in order to develop strength. They must encounter trials to see that they can overcome them. They must hear "no" so they know how to cope with it. Fortunately, Love and Logic allows us to provide these opportunities while at the same time providing loving encouragement and guidance. Love and Logic also makes a distinction between manageable struggles and overwhelming ones. Wise parents rescue their children from overwhelming difficulties. They allow their children to face the manageable ones.

- **"She has special needs. It's not fair to expect much."** When Chris and Amy were told that their soon-to-be-born daughter had Downs Syndrome, they felt as if they'd been hit by a truck. Nevertheless, they committed to ensuring that she would have the very best life possible. To them that meant doing everything for her and protecting her from every potential struggle. Now that she's a teen, their expectations for her are confirmed. She's incapable of doing much of anything. Sadly, she could have become so much more capable.

Love and Logic was largely developed with special needs children in mind. While there is no doubt that children with Downs Syndrome, Autism, ADHD, Sensory Processing Disorder, or other special needs require far more teaching, guidance, repetition, and patience from all of us, it's clear that most can achieve far more than many people believe.

Children will always live down-to or up-to the expectations we have for them. That's why we encourage parents of special needs children to establish fairly high ones—and then help their children learn to meet them. This means more practice brushing teeth, more practice following a list of pictures in order to get ready each morning, more practice tying their shoes, more practice saying "please" and "thank you," and more practice developing other practical coping skills.

We urge you to give them the repetitive practice they need before dramatically lowering your expectations. ◀

- **"If I provide any sort of discipline it will harm our attachment relationship."** Sierra did some "research" on the internet. From a few articles and blogs about attachment, she learned that four-year-old Colton must always feel nurtured and connected to her *all of the time*. This means that she must sleep with him each night, pay attention to him instead of completing conversations with her husband or anybody else, ensure that he receives enough soothing when he's having tantrums, and never spends any time in his room without her. She's now feeling confused and exhausted, because she was led to believe that this was how to raise a calm, well-adjusted child. Her Colton is not much fun to be around.

    Some wonderful books have been written on the subject of attachment and parenting. As you read in chapters 2 and 3 we understand that healthy adult-child attachment relationships form the foundation upon which all social, emotional, and intellectual health is built. There is nothing more important than consistently meeting our children's physical and emotional needs. There is nothing more important than developing and maintaining positive relationships with our children.

Some wacky stuff has also been written by people who misunderstand attachment and bonding. Much of it essentially suggests that the attachment relationship will suffer if we allow our children—or teens—to experience any type of limit or consequence that leaves them feeling unhappy for even a brief period of time. Ironically, people who try to apply this unwise advice actually create kids with propensities toward insecure attachment: When parents are frazzled with trying to meet every whim, how consistently nurturing will they be capable of being?

The key to raising securely attached and well-behaved children can be distilled into the following truth:

**Always meet their needs.
Set effective limits over their wants.**

Like our society in general, some authors have confused needs and wants.

- **"It worked for me!"** Thelma grew up in a traditional family, in a small town, at a time when the world was a lot simpler. She grew up feeling that her stern parents had done her a great favor by using angry lectures, threats, and spankings. Back then, children rarely considered disobeying their parents. Today, she's finding that anger and frustration don't work. She now spends most of her time feeling angry because her kids are sneaking around behind her back. The other day, her teenager cracked a smile as she was lecturing him about respect.

  There was a time in history when drill sergeant parenting was the style of choice. That's when our society was filled with far fewer choices and far more unstated yet powerful "social controls." Yes, there was a time when there was only one or two choices of shampoo, just about everyone got married at the same time in life—because that was "what you do," people got dressed up to go grocery shopping—because that was "what you do," young people gave their seats to older folks—because that was "what you do." Most people did most of what they did—because that was "what you do." Life was far simpler, and people were looked down upon if they didn't follow the unwritten rules of society.

Now we live in a societal free-for-all. The shampoo choices require an entire supermarket aisle, and our kids face an unlimited array of temptations. In contrast to decades past, rebellion is largely encouraged in our society, and the primary unwritten rule seems to be, "If it feels good do it!" There is also no such thing as "too much information" or basic modesty. Now our children can see and hear almost everything that's ever happened…no matter how tawdry…with the simple click of the mouse.

Our purpose here is not to provide social or cultural commentary. Our purpose is to simply state that young children today will soon be faced with making more life-and-death decisions than any group of young people during the entire course of human history. They will be faced with creating and following their own unwritten internal rules for living safely and ethically. If they don't receive plenty of practice making choices and experiencing the consequences, will they develop enough of these internal rules to thrive—or even survive—as they transition into adolescence and young adulthood?

- "I played video games growing up, and I'm okay." Curt grew up on a steady diet of Pong, Donkey Kong, Pac Man, and reruns of CHIPS. Erik Estrada was his favorite actor, and he now believes that video games and television actually helped him stay out of trouble as a kid. Because of this, he allows Krissie, his three-year-old, unlimited screen time. "She's so much happier when she can play with her tablet," he muses. "She reminds me of myself when I was a kid." ◄»

Today's video games, videos, and television are a far cry from what they were even five to ten years ago. So is the available research on what young children need in order to learn most effectively. The choice for all of us really comes down to the following:

Are we willing to settle for our children having okay brains or exceptional ones?

Many of today's screen-saturated children will turn out okay. They'll do okay in school and have okay relationships with others. They may find it unfulfilling to live life without being glued to the latest device, but the manufacturers will certainly be willing to provide the latest device…at a fair price, of course.

If you're taking the time to read this book, it's our guess that you would rather limit the screen time and give your child's brain an opportunity to become exceptional. "Exceptional" means packed with massive numbers of neural pathways devoted to self-control, creativity, problem solving, and overall social-emotional intelligence.

Seasoned preschool and kindergarten teachers can spot kids who spend lots of time interacting with loving adults—and very little time interacting with devices. One teacher puts it this way: "You can tell right away. Their eyes shine like brand new pennies. Nothing stops them. They're on fire for life, and they're only happy when they're learning and creating. They talk your leg off and never stop asking questions. They can be exhausting, but they blow you away with their creativity. You can't stop them. You just have to get out of their way and let them learn."

This same teacher described the other children she meets: "They just don't have the same spark or zest for life. In fact, many seem a bit lost or disconnected as they enter the room. Most of them are fairly well behaved and seem to be creative. That is until we discover that most of their "creativity" really involves them regurgitating the video games they play and the movies they watch. Most of them will be just fine."

Exceptional brain or okay one: It's your choice.

"My parents were Love and Logic parents, and they didn't even know it!" Jerry always wished his parents would yell at him or spank him. Instead, they expected him to solve his own problems and provided empathy before delivering consequences. He realizes now that they were strict, but loving at the same time. Jerry grew up not thinking much about how he was raised. All he knows is that parenting is almost automatic for him. For someone like Jerry, it's easy to avoid becoming a helicopter dad or drill sergeant.

Most parents want to raise great kids, and they have the best of intentions. Few people have the goal of raising irresponsible, nasty kids. Instead, almost everyone sets out to teach their children responsibility and show them love. How they choose to do it, however, can sure make a difference in how things turn out. Parents who want to make some changes can! We've seen it over and over again. How do they do it? They go slow by picking just one Love and Logic technique, experimenting with it, and seeing how it works. When they see some success, they move on and try another. That's why we have included the LOVE AND LOGIC EXPERIMENTS at the end of each chapter. These are great ways to get your feet wet. Take it slow, be patient with yourself, and have fun.

Caution!
Wise parents don't try every Love and Logic technique at once. Instead, they take it slow and experiment with one or two simple ideas at a time and have some fun.

There are no guarantees in life—no absolutely certain approaches to ensure that our children grow up to be lovable, kind, intelligent, reliable people. The odds are raised, however, when we start young and follow the two rules of Love and Logic. Let's review for a moment.

LOVE AND LOGIC RULE #1 FOR PARENTS:

**Remain a healthy role model.
Do this by setting limits and taking care
of yourself in loving, unselfish ways.**

- Act without frustration or anger.
- Stop using threats and repeated warnings.
- Set a limit once.
- Make statements you can enforce.
- Give kids a healthy sense of control.

LOVE AND LOGIC RULE #2 FOR PARENTS:

**Turn every mistake or misbehavior into
a learning opportunity.**

- Always provide a strong dose of empathy before delivering a consequence.
- Replace punishment with logical consequences.
- When possible, guide your child how to solve his or her own problem.

You don't have to be a perfect parent to raise a great kid!

Love and Logic Experiment #8

"Uh-oh. Looks like a little bedroom time."

Review Steps for the "Uh-Oh Song" on pages 88-90.

Give yourself plenty of planning time before trying this technique.

For at least two weeks, follow these steps exactly.

Remember: The best ways to sabotage this technique are to get frustrated and angry or to use too many words. Allow the consequence to do the teaching.

What should you do if your child cries and throws a major fit in the room?

The "Uh-Oh Song" is often harder for the parent than for the child. When he or she is throwing a fit in the room, say to yourself, "Sometimes we have to make our kids really upset in the short term so they can be happy and responsible in the long term."

Remember to have lots of fun with your kids when they are behaving well.

The "Uh-Oh Song" will not work unless the child loves to be with you so much that he or she misses you when alone in the room.

After two weeks, notice how your child responds to the words "Uh-oh!"

Parents all over the country tell us that their kids—as a result of this technique—learn to listen the first time, don't misbehave as much, and are a whole lot happier.

CHAPTER NINE

Potholes along the Road to Responsibility

It Can Be a Bumpy Road

Every journey has its obstacles, and every parent encounters problems with their children as they grow. Some of these problems are very small, whereas others are quite large and troubling. No matter how hard we have worked to smooth the way and to avoid the parental hazards, it's inevitable that we'll hit an occasional "pothole" along the way. ◀»

Some parents get stuck and sink forever into negative patterns with their children. Others fall into the very same holes yet quickly climb their way out. When we've fallen in, it can be very dark and difficult to see. Some parents refuse to admit to themselves or others that they've made some mistakes or that their young children are beginning to have problems. Others feel their way through the darkness, forgive themselves for their mistakes, take healthy action, and see their children blossom.

It can be challenging to admit when our children begin to fall into negative patterns. It can be even harder to admit that we're making some parenting mistakes. Be kind to yourself! Everyone makes them. We love our kids so much that we don't want to believe it when things aren't working. We all have dreams for how our children will turn out—they'll be happy, successful, have lots of friends, get married, and provide us with wonderful grandchildren. Is it scary when these dreams are threatened? Sure! What's the good news? First, nobody is asking you to be perfect. Imperfect parents have been known to raise wonderfully responsible and happy kids. Second, when we're brave enough to look at our mistakes, there are plenty of solutions to be found.

Common Potholes

Parents are biologically programmed to protect their young. Part of our "wiring," this programming drives us to meet their basic needs and shield them from harm. This, obviously, is a very good thing! Looking at the other side of the coin, this drive may also make it more difficult for us to admit that our children are beginning to learn some unhealthy habits. Clearly, it is human nature to make excuses for our children. We do this out of love. Sadly, some parents allow excuses to get in the way of making some changes that really need to happen early in a child's life. ◀)) The real tragedy is that behavior and personality problems get harder to correct with each year of a child's life. Young children are very flexible. They typically snap out of bad behavior quickly. I (Charles) have provided therapy to many families of older children and teens. What did I learn? Stated very simply, wise parents take simple actions early on so they can avoid having to take major, painful ones later in the child's life.

**Wise parents take simple actions early on
so they can avoid having to take painful ones later.
Pay now or pay later.**

The following are some common traps, or potholes, that many parents of young kids fall into. The first step is recognizing that anyone can fall into them. The second step is forgiving yourself if you have. The third step is experimenting with some Love and Logic solutions.

TRAP #1: *"He's just going through a phase."*

Little Malik is an energetic toddler who loves going to the grocery store with Mom. Why? Because he has more fun there than at the circus. He runs up and down the aisles, begs for candy, and revs his little engine while Mom goes bananas. "Malik? Get over here! Leave that alone. Don't go over there. If you grab that jar, you're not gonna get any candy. Wait 'til I tell your dad!" Malik is greatly entertained by his mother's exasperation, and he loves the attention he gets when she shouts.

In his travels throughout the store, Malik finds an unsuspecting victim. A grandfatherly gentleman is doing some shopping in the candy aisle. Soon, Malik is turning on the charm and begging him for a candy bar.

Malik's mother is searching for him. As she rounds the corner and sees what is happening, she screams, "MMMMMaaaaallllliiiik! Get over here! Leave that man alone!" Finally she grabs him by the arm, pulls him away, and says to the gentleman, "I'm so sorry. You know, he's going through one of those phases these days. He just won't listen to anything I say."

We're all concerned about Malik. What troubles us the most is the possibility that his mother might be saying the very same thing in ten or twelve years: "I'm so sorry, Officer. He's going through one of those phases these days. You know how teenagers are. He just won't listen to anything I say."

Malik's mom may not recall, when she looks back on her son's life, that this "phase" started as soon as he was able to hear her say "no." Children who are not taught early on to take "no" for an answer are the ones who don't know as teenagers how to "Just say no" to drugs, alcohol, and violence. By the time they reach their preteen or teen years, it might be too late to teach this lesson. When your toddler is "going through a phase" the only time to do something about it is right then.

What might Malik's loving mother try? First, we'd ask her to practice the "Uh-Oh Song" at home. Remember: Children are more likely to behave in public if this is locked in first at home. Second, we'd probably ask her to find a grocery store where the shopping carts have seat belts. Third, we'd suggest that she respond in this way as soon as he becomes wild: "Uh-oh, looks like a little cart time. This is so sad." Then we'd recommend she pick him up, put him in the cart, strap him in, and say to herself, "I didn't come to the store today to build a long-term relationship with these other shoppers. If I can keep my mouth shut and stay firm, life is going to get a lot better for everyone involved."

If Mom can take these steps, will both of their lives be better when Malik's fifteen? Absolutely! By the way, we know one mother who placed her child's car seat in the shopping cart. As soon as little Malik started to bellow in the store, Mom would sing, "Uh-oh. Looks like a little car seat time." It didn't take long before she got to leave the car seat in the car and enjoy a sweeter-acting Malik in the store. ◀

TRAP #2: *"Since we're together so much, she doesn't listen to a thing I say."*

Riley's teacher called Mom and asked her to come in for a parent–teacher conference. Riley came along too. While her mommy and her teacher sat in tiny plastic chairs and visited, she began noisily running around the room.

Her teacher looked over at her and said, "Riley, please come over here and sit with us." Riley walked right over and sat down. After about five minutes, she became bored, got up, and once again began running around the room.

This time it was Mom's turn. "Riley, come over here, okay?" Riley kept running. Turning to the teacher, Mom lamented, "We're together so much that she just won't listen to a word I say."

How would we respond if a preschool teacher argued, "I'm with these kids all day, so they just won't listen?" Probably just slightly better than a spouse who announces one evening, "Dear,

I'm with you so much that I just can't seem to listen or behave well for you. I just can't help it. You understand, don't you?"

All humor aside, don't fall into the trap of believing that spending a lot of time with your kids causes them to become "immune" to your discipline. Listed below are some experiments Riley's mom might try:

Love and Logic Experiments for Riley's Mom

1. **Use the "Uh-Oh Song."** Riley's mom might have sung, "Uh-oh, looks like a little time in the thinking chair," or, "Uh-oh, looks like time for you to sit in the hall so I can talk with your teacher."

2. **Have an "energy drain."** Mom might have delayed the consequence until that evening and said, "What a bummer. I was thinking of taking you to Silly Pete's Pizza, but after all of your running around while I was talking with your teacher, I don't have the energy."

3. **Try the "babysitter" routine.** "What a bummer," Mom says. "The conference was such hard work for me—I had to keep asking you not to run around—that I'm all worn out and need some relaxing time. Your dad and I are going out on a relaxation date tonight. How are you planning to pay your babysitter?"

TRAP #3: *"Other people let him do whatever he wants."*

Love and Logic parents believe that kids are smart enough to adapt to the different discipline styles of the adults they know. Children quickly learn to behave well for people who set and enforce solid, loving limits—and very poorly for those who don't. Love and Logic parents also believe it's a waste of valuable time and energy to blame other adults for their own children's misbehavior.

What's a parent to do if Grandma or Aunt Lucy or a divorced spouse does a lousy job of discipline while the kids are in their presence? As hard as it is to admit, the only thing we can actually control is how we behave—not how Grandma or Lucy or a divorced spouse behave. ◀»

Wise parents in this position grit their teeth, avoid blaming other adults in front of their kids, and spend most of their energy focusing on how they—themselves—can do the best parenting possible. In contrast, unwise parents spend most of their time and energy trying to control the uncontrollable—how other adults act around their kids. These parents soon find it impossible to stay positive and often begin to model lots of frustration, anger, and hopelessness in front of their kids.

> Dylan had just returned from a weekend at his father's house. Sitting at the dining room table with his mother, he started burping with great gusto.
>
> Mom, shocked by the display, reacted, "You stop that! That's bad manners. Cut it out right now!"
>
> Dylan burped again, because he immediately noticed how he could use this behavior to control his mommy. "Wow," he realized down deep, "look how red her face is getting. What fun!"
>
> "You stop that, young man!" Mom continued to lecture.
>
> Looking into her eyes, Dylan grinned a bit and said, "But Dad lets me."

Why is Dylan misbehaving? Is it because his father allows him to burp at the table? Not really. In the best of all worlds, Daddy would do a better job of setting limits over this issue, but do you suppose that Dylan can learn to behave better for his mother than for his father? Absolutely!

The true reason for Dylan's belching bonanza is his mother's reaction. Remember, anger and frustration feed misbehavior. The best way to make a nasty habit stick is by getting visibly upset and frustrated about it in front of your kids. How can Mom teach Dylan to save his gastric expressions for Dad's dinner table? Let's take a look at some Love and Logic experiments.

Love and Logic Anti-Belching Experiments

1. **"What a bummer. Dinner's over."** Mom might use an enforceable statement like, "I serve dinner to kids who use good manners at the table." As soon as Dylan belches— the very first time he does it—she takes his plate and says, "What a bummer. Dinner's over." Then she keeps her mouth shut and lets the empathy and consequence do the teaching.

2. **Encourage the behavior in another location.** She picks Dylan up, puts him in his room and says, "Here's a place where you can burp all you want. Burp as loud as you can in here. You can make your burps a lot better than you've been making them lately. Stay here and practice. Burp them all out. Come out as soon as they're gone."

When Dylan comes out, his mother sees that there's still a devilish look in his eyes. Smiling at him, she says, "Go back in there and burp some more. I can tell by the way your tummy is sticking out that you've got more in there. Come out when they are all gone." By the time Dylan comes out, he's pretty exhausted from all of this practice. As a matter of fact, he's ready for a nap.

3. **Have a disgust-induced "energy drain."** "Oh, Dylan," Mom says, "your burping drained the energy right out of me. How sad. Which of my chores are you going to do to recharge me?"

TRAP #4: *"What can you expect? She's only three."*

Some parents use age to excuse their children's misbehavior. "He's just so little. Give him a break." Love and Logic parents know young children can learn. They know young children can remember. Most importantly, they know that young children can learn and remember how to act nasty *or* learn and remember how to act nice. The choice is ours to make.

Olympia, who works at home, was in the middle of an important phone call. Sadly, her three-year-old kept interrupting her. "Mom! I need a drink of water! I want my puzzles. I can't reach them! Mom! Blow up this balloon! Mom! Mooommm!"

Olympia says into the phone, "I'm sorry. Can you repeat yourself? I didn't hear what you said." As the phone call continues, she keeps getting distracted by her daughter and having to ask the other person to repeat herself.

The woman on the other end of the line, hearing the entire commotion and getting quite irritated, asks, "Can you ask your child to stop for a moment so we can finish this call?" Rather insulted, Olympia replies, "She's just a little child. What do you expect?"

Some Love and Logic Experiments for Olympia

1. **The "Uh-Oh Song."** After the very first interruption, Mom might offer to call the person back, end the phone call, and sing, "Uh-oh, looks like a little bedroom time. You can come out as soon as you are calm and I've finished this call."

2. **Have an energy drain.** "How sad. All of these interruptions really tired me out while I was on the phone. Now I'm too tired to take you to the pool."

3. **Use the "Long, Long Phone Call" technique.** Olympia might call a friend and say, "I need to talk with you for

a long, long time." The more her daughter interrupts her while she is on the phone, the longer the phone call gets. She tells her daughter, "How sad. The more you interrupt me, the longer this is going to take."

Olympia might even stay on the phone after her friend hangs up. As soon as her child is quiet for two or three minutes, she hangs up and says, "When you're quiet it helps me finish my call. Thank you. I can get off the phone so much faster when you are quiet. I love you."

It doesn't take many long phone calls for a child to learn that it's smartest to leave Mom and Dad alone while they're talking.

TRAP #5: *"Sure she's a handful, but she's so creative—so intelligent!"*

Little Sara, along with lots of other kids, is enjoying a romp in the neighborhood swimming pool. Parents are watching as their kids have a great time. Sara starts teasing other kids, splashing them, taking their toys, pushing them off of their rafts, calling names, being bossy, and acting downright nasty. "This is my raft!" she complains to one child. "Nana nana boo boo. I got your ball. You can't get me," she teases another. "You're too slow, you big dummy," she says to another. How long is it going to take before Sara has no friends? How long will it be before every kid in the neighborhood starts to avoid her like the plague?

Watching with another parent, Sara's dad smiles and says, "She can really be a challenge, but she's so intelligent and creative. I just don't think that other kids can understand her. She's so bright. She's just on another level."

It's difficult to understand why some of us fall into this trap with our kids. Perhaps because it's a whole lot easier to see our children as creative and misunderstood than obnoxious and irritating? Perhaps it also has something to do with the "tortured artist" stereotype. For some reason, our society has come to associate creativity with irresponsibility. Where did this begin? It seems that all one has to do, if one wants to get away with being rude or nasty, is to claim genius or say, "I'm just expressing my creative talents." What's the real truth about this? Even the most creative and intelligent people find it difficult to succeed unless they can get along with others and be responsible members of society. ◄》

A Love and Logic Solution for Sara's Dad

Leave the fun activity. Whenever our kids misbehave at the pool, the park, a friend's house, a movie theater, or some other place they want to be, the decision is simple. Without giving repeated warnings, without lectures, and without anger and frustration, Dad needs to say something like, "Oh no. This is so sad, Sara. Looks like swimming is over for today."

I (Charles) recently went to the movie theater with my son. As the movie began, I noticed two kids throwing popcorn and creating quite a commotion. Sadly, I also noticed their mother and father giving them about fifteen warnings to stop. What does the Love and Logic parent do? As the first popcorn kernel flies, the parent says, "Please pick that up and throw it away. We will be leaving if I see you continue to misbehave." As the second kernel flies, the parent says, "What a bummer. Guess it's time to go home." Then he or she follows through with actions instead of words. We do our kids a great disservice by giving them repeated warnings. Set the limit once and follow through.

Potholes along the Road to Responsibility
• "He's just going through a phase."
• "Since we're together so much, she just won't listen to me."
• "Other people let him do whatever he wants."
• "What do you expect? She's just a little child."
• "She's just so creative. Other people just can't understand."
• "I tell him and I tell him, but he just won't listen."

TRAP #6: *"I tell him and I tell him, but he just won't listen."*

When we hear parents say, "I tell him and I tell him," we're already starting to get a clue about what might be going wrong. The parent is relying on words instead of actions. Said differently, the parent has fallen into the trap of believing that more warnings, lectures, threats, or arguing will solve the problem. What do kids learn the most from? Do they learn the most from our words? Or, instead, do they learn the most from our actions? We keep saying it: Actions speak louder than words.

> Isaac is in the middle of another free-for-all with his mother at the lunch table. With a twisted little face, he demands, "I want a cookie!"
>
> Mom replies, "You can have one after you eat your carrots."
>
> "But why?" Isaac whines. "Dad said I don't have to."
>
> "If you don't eat your vegetables, you're going to get sick!" Mom explains.
>
> "Tony eats candy for lunch and he's okay," Isaac continues to argue.
>
> This makes the veins on Mom's forehead bulge. "I'm telling you no! I mean it! For crying out loud, eat those carrots or you can forget about sweets!"
>
> Isaac mumbles, "You hate me."
>
> Feeling a twinge of guilt, Mom replies, "How many times do I have to tell you? I love you. That's why you need to eat your carrots. There are plenty of starving kids around who would be thankful for them."
>
> Isaac grins, "They can have them. Send 'em to them."
>
> "That's not funny. You eat those. I paid good money for them. We don't waste food around here." And so on.

What a bummer for both Isaac and his mom. The only real solution for this one is to stop the arguing. Easier said than done? Just wait until you read the next section. Are you ready for a foolproof strategy for ending arguing and back talk? Would you like to hear how Mom learned how to handle Isaac without breaking a sweat? If so, read on.

Arguing for Fun and Profit

Does it ever feel like kids today carry around a little manual called "Arguing for Fun and Profit"? Do you ever get tired of hearing phrases like "But why?" or "Not fair!" or "You hate me!" or "Mom lets me!" or "If you really loved me, you would let me."? Where does all of this back talk come from anyway?

Many children learn at an early age that arguing has some payoffs. What it can win them, first of all, is an exciting show of parental frustration and anger. Many children "hook" their parents with something like, "Not fair!" Then they sit back, watch, and think to themselves, "Wow! Look at me! I'm just a little kid, but I can change the color of Dad's face, the tone of Mommy's voice, maybe even the potential longevity of their cardiovascular systems!" Might this be what's happening between Isaac and his mom?

Secondly, some children learn that arguing wears their parents down and will eventually cause their parents to back down. They learn that if they nag, annoy, and pester long enough, their parents will give in.

Research on kids with major behavior problems—kids, for example, who've been in trouble with the law—shows that one of the best predictors of a child having these problems is his or her ability to pull adults into power struggles and arguments. What does this mean? Teaching your kids that arguing does not work is one of the most important things you will ever do.

The way we determine how a child sucks us into a power struggle is to ask ourselves if we do any, or all, of the following:

- **Use too many threats that we can't back up.** "If you don't stop that right now, you're going to be sorry. I mean it! You stop it now! Wait 'til your dad gets home! Be nice!"

- **Try to reason with a child when he or she talks back.** "The reason you shouldn't use language like that is because I'm your parent and I'm older, and you need to respect me. Oh! Now you think this is funny! Wipe that smile off your face!"

- **Get frustrated, angry, or give in to a child's demands.** "Okay, you can have Pop Tarts, just this once, but don't you ever ask me for them again!" ◄»

Neutralizing Family Arguments

Are you ready for the fun part? Are you ready for a time-tested, proven, anti-argue approach? Listed below are some of the Love and Logic steps that can get parents off the hook when their kids begin playing "verbal brain drain."

STEP 1: Go "brain dead," smile, and pause. Going "brain dead" means we don't think about what the child has just said. If we do, we might unwittingly show some anger, and our child, knowing we've been affected, will continue the misbehavior. Instead, our goal is to take a stance that shows we're in control of ourselves and can handle the child without breaking a sweat.

What does this stance look like? First, smile or look at the child with love in your eyes. Second, pause. Hold this pause until your child says, "What?" Children often learn very quickly—if a parent is consistent—that when Mom smiles and pauses, arguing isn't going to work.

STEP 2: Choose an empathetic "one-liner." Choose an empathetic "one-liner" from the "Love and Logic One-Liner" chart. "One-liners" can be very effective, only if they are delivered with genuine compassion and understanding.

STEP 3: Keep repeating the same "one-liner" over and over. Repeat your "one-liner" over and over again, with sadness instead of anger. "I love you too much to argue" has proven to be one of the easiest and most effective. Whispering the statement often makes this technique even more powerful.

STEP 4: If the child continues, walk away. If he follows, you may have to resort to changing his location or having a severe energy drain. A father we knew used to say this: "What a bummer. Arguing drains energy. What are you going to do to charge me up? You can tell me tonight. Try not to worry."

Some Sample Love and Logic One-Liners

The Child	You Say
"But why?"	"Why do you think?"
"I hate you!" or "You hate me."	"I'm sorry you feel that way."
"Dad lets me."	"I know."
"Not fair!"	"I'll listen to you when your voice sounds like mine."
Just about anything your child might say:	"I love you too much to argue."

Remember Isaac, the child who wanted a cookie? Here's how things changed with just a little Love and Logic magic.

"Isaac," his mother says, "feel free to have a cookie after you eat your carrots."

"But why?" Isaac complains. "Dad said that I don't have to." His mother pauses, smiles, and waits for Isaac to respond. "What!?" Isaac whines.

His mom looks at him, smiles sweetly, and whispers, "I love you too much to argue."

"So I don't have to eat my carrots?" Isaac asks.

Still smiling, his mother says, "You can have a cookie after you eat them."

"But why?"

His mother pauses again and smiles, then waits for Isaac to respond.

"But I want the cookie now!"

Maintaining her sweetness, his mother says, "I love you too much to argue."

"You hate me!" Isaac responds.

"I love you too much to argue," his mother says.

"I want it now! I hate you!" Isaac cries.

His mother begins to sing, "Uh-oh. Looks like a little bedroom time…"

By now, Isaac knows what this means.

❤ ❤ ❤

Did you notice how this technique can make a child really angry? Why do kids get angry? Because they're not getting their way—they're losing control. Unhealthy control. One of the keys to great parenting is giving away healthy control—control within limits—while taking away unhealthy control, control that damages relationships.

**Sometimes we have to make our kids
really mad in the short term, so they can be
happier and more responsible
in the long term.**

A week later, Isaac wanted a video on his mom's laptop. Here's what happened.

"I want to watch *Mutant Death Squad*."

"You may color instead, honey," his mom said.

Mom smiled, paused, and waited for Isaac to respond. In a moment, he slumped down in his seat, crossed his arms and said, "Don't say it!" he said. "I know. You love me too much to argue."

❤ ❤ ❤

Are you guessing that Isaac's mom is now a much happier woman? What's really exciting is that Isaac, overall, is now a much happier kid.

Love and Logic Experiment #9

Putting an End to Arguing

*Review the steps for neutralizing arguments
on page 175.*

Remember: Young children who learn that arguing works for them become teenagers and adults who are really unpleasant to be around.

*Review how Mom dealt with Isaac's arguing
on page 173.*

Notice how Mom kept repeating, "I love you too much to argue."

*Memorize the words,
"I love you too much to argue."*

Every time your child begins to argue, respond with this very same statement.

Expect this to make your child really mad.

Most children get very angry when their parents start using this technique.

*Notice how much more energy you have
at the end of the day.*

It's amazing how fast arguing drains the energy out of us. Take good care of yourself—and your child—by putting an end to it early in his or her life.

CHAPTER TEN

The Power
of Chores

Chores Build Responsibility and a Healthy Sense of Self

I (Charles) was hired by a school district to speak with teachers about classroom management. The evening before my presentation, one of the teachers from the school picked me up at the airport. She brought along her teenage son, Joe. As we walked through the airport, I couldn't help but notice what a nice kid he was. He held doors open for us and said strange things such as "please" and "thank you." As we walked by a store in the airport, he asked his mother to buy him something. She simply said, "No."

I was shocked by his response. "Okay," he said. No arguing, no back talk, and no "attitude."

"Wait a minute!" I thought to myself. "This has got to be a dream. When am I going to wake up?" I pinched myself and realized that what had just happened was actually real.

The next day, this same teacher drove me back to the airport. This time her son did not come along. Seizing the opportunity, I asked, "Your son, Joe, seems to be one of the nicest teenagers I've met in a long time. What have you done? What are you feeding that kid?"

Without reservation or hesitation, she answered, "Chores."
"What?" I asked.

Again she answered, "Chores. We started feeding him chores when he was three." That was her explanation.

I wasn't surprised. For decades we've seen the same thing: Children who contribute to the family in the form of chores—without being nagged or paid to complete them—become far more respectful, responsible, and motivated people.

Has this mother given Joe something that's been missing in the lives of many kids today? Yes! When we compare children who grew up during the Great Depression with those who are growing up now, one difference is clear. Kids who grew up then had to struggle in order to survive. Times were extremely hard for most families. Kids grew up with a sense of purpose and a sense of being valued and needed by their families. They also grew up believing they could accomplish almost anything if they worked hard enough. As a result, most became very responsible adults with relatively healthy levels of confidence and strength to persevere.

- Chores show kids they are valued and needed.
- Chores help develop responsibility and respect for authority figures.
- Chores build healthy confidence and the strength to keep going when the going gets tough.
- Completing chores creates strong feelings of satisfaction. ◀))

When economic times were even tougher for many people, everyone in the family had to pitch in. Children learned early on that hard work and perseverance were simply "the things that good folks do." Most saw, first hand, that they were needed and highly valued members of the family team. Today, we as a society, steal these good feelings from our children by expecting them to contribute so little. We've forgotten this age-old truth:

**Serving others is a blessing for those
who serve—not just those being served.**

Now, many of our youth attempt to self-medicate loneliness, lack of purpose, and low confidence by overusing or abusing video games, the internet, and other activities/substances. Some even join gangs, cults, or terrorist groups to meet their need to belong and to contribute.

The Formula for a Healthy Sense of Self and a Happier Life

To achieve a strong, healthy sense of self—to achieve reasonable happiness in life—children have to: (1) try some things that are challenging; (2) struggle; (3) receive encouragement from those they love; (4) experience effort-related success; (5) have adults who focus on their effort *not* their intelligence.

Struggling with difficult tasks, or tasks that seem too hard at first glance, is an essential part of building a strong sense of self. How do we feel when we try something we don't believe we can do, stick with it, achieve success, and look back on our accomplishment? The answer is simple. We feel great about ourselves.

A friend of ours took up mountain climbing. She was terrified by the prospect of hanging hundreds of feet above the ground by a single rope. As she struggled with her fear, enjoyed some success, and reflected on what she had done, she developed a higher level of respect for herself—and high quality climbing ropes!

Sadly, our society has become confused about what makes people happy. Many of us have forgotten that happiness comes from doing great things—rather than getting great things. So, the true formula for high self-concept does not involve giving your children a lot of things that they want. It doesn't involve making them happy all of the time. It doesn't even involve telling them they are great on a daily basis. Instead, the true recipe involves giving the gift of struggle, letting them work through challenging tasks and problems, providing encouragement and unconditional love, and allowing them to take pride in their accomplishments.

In short, kids feel good when they work hard and accomplish good things. Chores are an excellent way to make this happen.

Struggle + Encouragement from others + Accomplishment + Others focusing on effort = Healthy Sense of Self ◀»

In the first edition of this book, we failed to emphasize the critical importance of focusing on children's effort, instead of how bright they are. Please don't make the tragic mistake of saying to your children:

- "You did that. You are so smart!"
- "You are so bright. You figured it out."
- "You did that so well. You are so intelligent!"

While these all sound like nice things to say to a child, they set children up for eventual failure and great distress. Why? The reason has to do with the fact that "smartness" and "brightness" and "intelligence" are static—uncontrollable traits. Since children who've been praised this way cannot change their IQ's, they experience great pain when they encounter things they cannot excel at immediately. Since nobody enjoys pain, they quickly learn to give up. As they grow, they also become adept at avoiding anything challenging that might interfere with being viewed as smart, bright, or intelligent.

Wiser parents comment on their children's success by saying things like:

- "You did that. You kept trying even when it got challenging."
- "You worked a long time on that. You figured it out."
- "You did that so well. You are such a hard worker."

Even though children who've heard these things can't change their IQ's, they can change their level of effort or perseverance.

As a result, these children don't take failures as the end of the world. They simply reason that success takes a bit more hard work. Therefore, these are the children who are far more likely to try more challenging things and to remain motivated even when they face difficulties.

Let's now move on from the somewhat theoretical to the very practical: How does a parent get their kids to do chores…so that they can experience this formula for strong sense of self and happiness?

Getting Your Kids to Do Chores

Let's take a look at some healthy ways of giving your children the gift of struggle, through chores.

STEP 1: *As soon as your child can walk, start working together.*

- Play together and work together. Have fun together. Wash dishes, clean sinks, dust furniture, sweep, and so on.
- Say "please" and "thank you" so your kids are encouraged to say them, too.
- Do your best to help your child learn to associate chores with good feelings rather than bad ones.
- Do not criticize quality. Instead, focus mostly on the amount of effort your child expends. "Wow! You're really working hard!"

STEP 2: *Model doing your own chores in front of your kids.*

- Make sure your kids see you doing chores, working hard, struggling.
- Make sure they see how good you feel once the chores are done—your sense of completion and accomplishment.
- Think out loud as you work. Say things like, "This is hard. All right, I've got to do it. It has to get done. Okay, I'm doing it now. Wow, I'm almost finished. It's done! Boy, do I feel great now!"

- It's important for children to know that we sometimes have to work hard at tasks we don't necessarily like. Lying and saying that all chores are fun, when they're really not, only creates frustration and resentment within your child later on. Be positive, but honest. ◄))

STEP 3: *Develop a "Toy Bermuda Triangle."*

- When your young child leaves toys lying around and doesn't put them away, as requested, where do the toys go? To the Toy Bermuda Triangle!
- "Where are my toys?" your child asks. How do you respond? "When you pick up your toys, you get to keep them. When I pick up your toys, they go in my closet. How are you going to earn them back?"

STEP 4: *Give choices about age-appropriate chores.*
Remember not to say, "Do it now."

- Offer your child a choice of chores. Your child must choose between two chores, each of which are okay with you. "Would you like to dust the baseboards in the house, or would you like to pull weeds in the backyard?"
- Instead of always saying, "Do it now!" give away some control by allowing your child to choose between two deadlines. "Would you like to do the chore now, or have it done by 3 p.m.? I'll show you what 3 p.m. looks like on the clock."
- Giving your child some time to complete the chore also gives you some time to plan what you will do if he or she forgets or refuses to do it. When we say, "Do it now!" we are really in a bad place if our kids say, "No!"

STEP 5: *Do not pay your children for doing chores.*

- Chores are a contribution to the family. Nobody gets paid for doing them.
- When your child asks, "What am I going to get for doing this?" your response is, "There's no pay for chores. Chores are part of being a family." These are everyday chores, such as doing dishes, helping with the laundry, dusting, cleaning, picking up today, etc. ◀))

Example: A parent can take an old sock, put it over a child's hand, spray a little polish or dusting solution on the sock, and let the child do some dusting.

Example: A parent can ask a child to put away the silverware. Kids enjoy putting the forks where the forks go and the spoons where the spoons go—into a dishwasher or a silverware drawer.

Example: After their clothes come out of the laundry, you can show them how to fold them, and they can put them away in the proper drawer.

Example: Another good chore is cleaning the bathroom sink when a child is done using it. Parents can wet a rag and demonstrate how it's done. Parents and kids can do it together.

**Keep in mind that
when children are very young,
the quality of the chore isn't
as important as the effort.
Also, please remember to say,
"Thank you!"**

- When a child wants to earn something—money, a special activity, or a toy—a parent can say, "If you want to earn money, you can find some extra things that I would normally do. I will be happy to pay you when they are finished and done well."

STEP 6: *Hope your kids, when they're still very young, forget or refuse to do their chores.*

- Do not remind your kids to do their chores. Pray they will forget. Why? So they can learn early how to get tasks done without constant reminders or nagging.
- When a child forgets to do a chore, say to yourself, "The road to wisdom is paved with mistakes. Boy, is my child getting wise this week!"
- Do the chore for your child, or hire somebody to do it. Then, approach your child and say, "How sad. Remember when I asked you to pick up your clothes and you didn't? I love you too much to remind you. I took care of it. How are you going to pay me?"

When a child says, "I don't know," try the steps we learned in Chapter 7:

1. Lock in the empathy.
2. Say, "What are you going to do?"
3. When your child doesn't know, ask, "Would you like some ideas?"
4. Provide a menu of options:
   - "Want to hear what others have done?"
   - "Some kids decide to…" (fill in the blank)
   - "How would that work for you?"
5. Allow your child to choose, and learn from the choice.

How do we prepare our kids for life, for those times when an employer asks them to do something? Do we prepare them by giving them plenty of reminders, or by teaching them to do things the first time they're asked? Give your kids a distinct advantage over most of their workforce peers. How? Teach them to do chores without reminders.

Something interesting happens when we worry that our children will make mistakes. When they sense our insecurity and anxiety, they usually confirm our greatest fears. On the other hand, when we look forward to their mistakes, because we know the road to wisdom is paved with them, our kids can sense this too. What happens? When they sense our confidence, they actually tend to make smarter decisions. It's almost as if they reason, "Wow. Mom is so self-assured. She's not worried a bit. I wonder what's up her sleeve."

**Strange as it seems,
children wind up making far fewer mistakes
when we no longer fear that they will.** ◄»

Applying appropriate consequences when kids forget or refuse to do their chores is one of the most powerful Love and Logic tools. We love when our kids forget or refuse to do their chores at an early age—when the price tag is small. This means by the time they're teens, or adults, these lessons will have already been learned.

The mother of that wonderfully polite and respectful teenager, Joe, told us that even though her son had never liked doing the chores he was given, when he finished, she'd always notice a look of satisfaction on his face. He would never admit to liking the chores, but he always seemed proud of himself for having done the job. She also told us that even though he's now 6'5" tall, an inch taller than his father, he said to her recently, "I know that I'm taller than Dad now, but why does he still seem bigger?"

She said she just smiled at him and didn't answer, because she didn't know what to say. What is the answer? Simply stated, Joe's mother and father proved to him early on that they could be strict yet loving at the same time. When parents establish themselves as loving authority figures during the first three years of life, they will forever seem "big" or important in the eyes of their children—no matter how big or how old their children get.

We have had the great joy of learning a lot from all of the people we meet at our conferences. Earl was a wise man who attended a Love and Logic conference we held in the Southwest. An older gentleman, he was dressed like a cowboy. As he approached us, we noticed his friendly smile and his weathered skin. The many wrinkles in his face surely told of many a day riding horses under the blistering desert sun.

Offering a handshake, he remarked, "I've known this stuff for a long time. I do it with my horses."

I (Jim) asked jokingly, "You mean, 'How sad' and 'What a bummer'?"

"No! Not that part," he smiled. "When they're still small, I show 'em I can be kind and real strong at the same time. When they're still real small, I get down and play with 'em, wrestle with 'em and move 'em around. They grow to love me, but they also know I'm gonna be in charge. The best part is this. When they get to be four times bigger than I am, and they could squash me in a heartbeat, they still think I'm bigger than they are. It's great. When it comes time to break 'em, it's a whole lot easier. I don't have to work so hard, and it's easier for them, too.

"When I get up on the horse," he continued, "it struggles a bit but mellows out darn fast. Now, my neighbor down the road don't spend much time with his horses until they're big. What a show when he goes to break 'em. They start buckin' and brayin' and carrying on. It's painful to watch."

❤ ❤ ❤

Should we start when our kids are small—playing, setting limits, bonding, and providing discipline? Or should we wait until they are big and try to "break" them later? You know the answer.

Thank you for reading this book. You have just given your children a gift that will last their entire lives—and the lives of their children!

> Parents who establish themselves
> as loving authority figures early
> in their children's lives, create the foundation
> for a lifelong relationship of respect,
> trust, and love.

Love and Logic Experiment #10

Building Responsibility and a Strong Sense of Self with Chores

Review the steps for Getting Your Kids to Do Chores on pages 185-187.

After reviewing these steps, pick two chores that are appropriate for your child.

Describe each chore to your child and let him or her make a choice.

Start by having your child pick one chore. Why do we suggest giving a choice? Simply because the odds of your child being cooperative go up when you offer one. If your child doesn't choose within ten seconds flat, make the choice yourself.

*Once a chore is chosen, start by working together
and having lots of fun.*

The goal here is to build positive feelings about helping out
around the house. Caution! Focus on your child's effort, avoid
criticizing, and focus on the positive.

*Gradually shift responsibility onto your child
for completing this chore.*

Little by little, expect your child to do more and more of the
chore without you. Eventually, let your child know he or she is
"big enough" to do the chore independently.

*If your child refuses or forgets, do not warn,
nag, or remind.*

Children need to learn how to complete tasks without their
parents standing over them 100 percent of the time. Children
also need to learn how to complete tasks without being nagged,
reminded, or warned.

When your child refuses or forgets to do the chore, do it
for him or her. Then say something like, "What a bummer. You
forgot to do your chore. I love you too much to nag you, so I
did it. How are you planning to pay me for my time?"

Gradually add more chores as your child grows.

CHAPTER ELEVEN

Bedtime

Two-year-old Liam wailed, "No bedtime! No! I not tired!" "No sleep!"

By eight o'clock each evening his parents had lost their parenting skills, "Get back in your room! It's bedtime! How many times do we have to tell you? Get back in your bed and go to sleep!"

Liam went to plan B, "But I scared! I scared!"

While suspecting a con job, Mom and Dad felt conflicted… and guilty. "Maybe he is terrified," they wondered. Dutifully trudging back to his room they tried to be good parents like their friends on social media, "There's nothing to be afraid of, Liam. We are just down the hall."

"I need a hug. Lay with me, Mommy."

By this time of night Mom was a crispy and vacant shell of a mom. Broken from the water torture, she relented, "Well, okay. If you stay in your bed, I'll lie with you… but just for a while."

"What is happening? I can't sleep!" yelled six-year old Emily, Liam's sister sib. "I can't find Whiskers! He's lost! Whiskers is lost! I can't sleep without him."

"Did you look between your bed and the wall?" Dad moaned. "He's got to be in there."

"Daddy! He's gone!"

Pushed well past the limits of sanity, Dad responded with enough volume to wake the entire block, "For crying out loud! He's a stuffed animal. He couldn't have run away! We'll find him in the morning. Go to sleep!"

Bedtime with young children is not for the faint of heart. Many loving parents have found themselves regretting the way they've handled it, while feeling unsure about what else to do. Fortunately, Love and Logic offers tried and true strategies for turning this often tumultuous event into a tender and happy one.

The First Year

Babies are amazing communicators. They have to be. Their physical and emotional lives depend on it.

As we discussed in Chapter Three, the first year of life is all about needs. That's why we never recommend allowing a very young child to simply "cry it out." Instead, we urge parents and other caregivers to promptly assume the detective role, diligently searching for clues. Why is this little one crying? What's the underlying need? Sometimes the issue is obvious, a little food… a diaper change… some cuddling… or some other relatively simple measure does the trick. Other times, identifying the need takes some deeper investigation, as it might involve pain associated with an ear infection, teething, or something else.

Remember three basic truths:

- The first year of life is about establishing trust and healthy attachment

- When they cry, do whatever it takes to meet their needs
- Meeting their needs at night is the best way to help them develop good sleeping habits for when they become toddlers... and teens

What a precious and exhausting time. It's precious because we don't have to bother our heads over issues like teaching responsibility, dealing with homework, or helping them with peer pressure. Oh, how sweet it is that we can spend our time simply loving them and cuddling and gazing into their beautiful eyes!

It's an exhausting time because... well... it requires a lot of sleepless nights to meet the needs of someone who can't meet their own. As time goes by, however, the bond this creates will prove priceless.

Toddlers and Preschoolers

As their first birthday nears, life changes dramatically. It changes for them and it changes for us. In addition to their long list of needs, they also develop an equally large assortment of desires. Like scientists, they begin to run a variety of experiments, each designed to gather data about our ability to set limits and maintain a calm and healthy home.

During their first year, they learn to trust us by seeing that we always meet their needs.

During the second year and beyond, this basic process continues. Another also emerges, when they begin to wonder, "Do my parents love me enough to provide limits? Are they strong enough to keep me safe from my own unhealthy desires?"

The only way for a child to know with certainty this is the case is to run plenty of experiments. Of course, this testing doesn't involve them writing an intentional plan. It's almost exclusively subconscious and automatic. Nevertheless, the results will have a dramatic impact on their behavior and sense of self.

One of the most basic and common experiments involves seeing if I, the toddler, am capable of running the home after bedtime. Discussed below are some tips for calmly addressing this test… and thus giving our kids the security of knowing that we have what it takes to provide the loving leadership they need.

Establish a consistently calming routine

Without some level of consistency and predictability our lives quickly become overwhelming and anxiety laden. Imagine living in a busy city where traffic rules changed almost daily without notice. On some days red lights signaled stop. On other days they meant go. Sometimes the directionality of one-way streets would suddenly reverse. So would the side of the road drivers were required to travel.

Sometimes even the most loving and competent parents occasionally slip out of providing predictable and consistent evening routines. When they do so, they notice plenty of fender benders, anxiety, and even road rage as they attempt to get their little ones settled down for the night. Small children are a bit like high-performance cars with under-developed steering and braking systems. They need a predictable course and plenty of time to make turns and to slow themselves down.

Each evening a gradual slow-down is the goal. As the minutes pass, wise parents set the tone by lowering the lights, their voices, and the general tempo of their homes. They also do their best to provide the same sequence of events each evening. For example, first comes dinner, then we take a bath, then we read a story, then we hug and kiss and say our prayers, and so on.

Predictability = Safety = Love = Calm

Minimize Screen Time

This is so important that it deserves its own section! Even earlier in the day, young children should have very little screen time. Why? Simply because time spent in front of screens (including phones, tablets, or any other digital devices) is time away from the activities essential for healthy brain and body development. Little children learn by doing. They learn by being talked to. They learn from babbling sounds, babbling words, and eventually expressing themselves in quite exciting and often entertaining sentences, paragraphs, and multi-volume book sets. They learn by interacting with loving adults who smile, laugh, rock them on their knees, and push them on swings. They learn by actively and physically exploring their worlds. They learn by getting dirty and making messes, and they learn by tossing their clothes in the washer as well as by helping us clean up their messes.

Evenings need to be calm times where children experience calm words, calm touch, and people who yawn a good amount of the time. Since young ones take their emotional cues from the leaders in the home, we are smart to remain such leaders… rather than allowing screens to assume that role.

Digital technology over-stimulates. Calm adults help regulate.

Model Calm Confidence

Bedroom time goes much smoother when parents take a hint from successful airline pilots. These great professionals know how to communicate without emitting a hint of apprehension or unease. Perfecting the slow mumble, they share the facts in ways that leave passengers strangely relaxed.

Imagine you are in an airplane about to land during a major upper Midwest blizzard. Wind shear is buffeting the plane with gale force winds. Outside the window you see nothing but snow and realize you are about to land in a complete whiteout—you begin to fear that the runway might be icy. The speaker above your head cracks to life. It's the pilot making his ultra-relaxed and slightly mumbled announcement:

We're beginning our final decent into Frostbite Falls International Airport. Fasten your seat belts, as the ride is going to be just a bit bumpy. We'll have you on the ground in about 5 minutes. Thanks for flying with us.

People take their emotional cues from others around them. This essential leadership truth has been understood for hundreds… if not thousands of years. Supporting this principle is recent research documenting the existence of so called "mirror neurons." These wonderful nerve cells allow us to mirror the emotions of those around us, contributing to a sense of empathy and connectedness.

The question for all of us is this:

In our home, who is rubbing off on whom?

Especially during bedroom time, children need caregivers who can communicate like highly-skilled 737 pilots. This means using a calm and confident voice and resisting the urge to get pulled into debates. To make this point, let's consider two different parents handling a three-year-old claiming monster invasion:

Parent A:

    Child: "I can't go to bed. There's monsters!"

    Parent (shining a flashlight under the bed): "See… there are no monsters."

    Child: "They went in my closet."

    Parent (directing the light into the closet): "There are no monsters there. Honey, it's okay. There are no monsters."

    Child (fearful): "Yeah but they behind my door."

    Parent (frustrated and feeling insecure): "They are not. See? There are no monsters. You are safe. You are going to have a great night. There is nothing to be afraid of."

Parent B:

Child: "I can't go to bed. There's monsters!"

Parent (with kindness, but almost no emotion): "Aren't you glad that monsters aren't real?" (as these words leave their lips, they are giving a kiss on the cheek and moving quickly out of the child's room.)

Which of the parents above has sent a message of calm confidence? Which has not? Which communicated through their many words and their flashlight that monsters might actually exist? Which has remained a strong leader whose calm demeanor is likely to rub off on her children?

Change "bedtime" into "Bedroom time"

The best way to wake a young child is to lecture them about how tired they are. The best way to start an unwinnable power struggle is to dictate that a young child remain in their bed with their head resting on their pillow.

Even the most skilled parent cannot make their child fall asleep. That's why we strongly recommend saying to the child:

It's bedroom time. You may do whatever you want in here as long as it doesn't become a problem for anyone else in the family.

Love and Logic is dedicated to helping parents avoid getting mired in relationship-damaging power struggles. It's also committed to helping kids develop self-control and personal responsibility. If we spend our energy attempting to micromanage when our kids fall asleep, might we end up someday having a teen or young adult who believes that the best way to rebel is to stay out all night? Instead, will we enjoy a far happier and more self-controlled youth if they learn from experience that lack of sleep makes for a very miserable day?

Like everything else, young children learn how to regulate their own sleep through the natural processes of maturation and the three E's of Love and Logic:

- Learning from our **E**xample that healthy people take care of their bodies and minds.
- Learning from **E**xperience that it's no fun to be exhausted.
- Learning these lessons from us because we use **E**mpathy rather than anger.

Provide Shared Control Within Limits

Well-timed choices can make all of the difference. "Well-timed" means these tiny choices are given prior to our kids getting resistant, not after. Choices provided before resistance share healthy control within limits. Those given afterward reward resistance.

Examples include asking five minutes prior to bedroom time, "Do you want to start bedroom time now... or in five minutes?"

Other examples are:

- "Would you rather have your light on or off?"
- "Do you want your teddy bear, your bunny, or both?"
- "Will you be sleeping with your head at the top of the bed or at the bottom?"

Yes! It's okay to have fun with this. That is, as long as we remember to provide only those options that we're happy with. Even more examples include:

- Will you be sleeping on top of your covers or below them?
- Do you want your Spider Man pajamas or your red ones?
- Are you going to go to sleep right away or in a little while?
- Do you want a story or no story?
- Will you be sleeping on the floor or in your bed?
- Do you think it would be best to sleep lying down or standing up?

We have been asked, "Are you really serious about letting a toddler decide when they go to sleep?"

Our answer is always the same, "Absolutely!" When parents take this little leap of faith, they almost always find their lives become a lot less stressful, and their kids learn to self-regulate. That is, as long as they (the parents) commit to enforcing bedroom time by expecting their kids remain in the rooms.

Enforce bedroom time

"How do I keep them in their bedroom?" Astute parents are quick to ask this question. Answering it requires that we first remember to apply great doses of two precious commodities: Love and common sense. Both of these remind us to always respond when our children have needs that must be met. This decision is easiest, clearest cut, when our babies are younger than toddling age. When they cry, we take care of them.

As we mentioned in Chapter Three, when we're not sure whether our child is demonstrating a need or a want, we are always wise to err on the side of assuming there is a need. It's impossible to traumatize a young child by providing too much love and nurturing. It is possible to cause serious damage by consistently failing to meet needs.

When it becomes clear that our child is crying or acting out because they *want* to roam the home or *want* to sleep with us parents, many people decide to provide loving boundaries by expecting that their child stay in their room. "I allow kids to have their doors open as long as they stay in their rooms" sets the limit. Continuing to return them to their bedroom, and perhaps holding the door shut when they try to exit, enforces the limit. Make sure that the room is safe and that you or some other loving adult remains just outside of the door.

Sometimes it helps to remind ourselves that the more consistently we enforce this limit, the quicker our child will learn to remain in their room without becoming upset or throwing a tantrum. Training also happens faster when we avoid lectures, threats, trying to reassure them or backing down. Every extra word we use causes our child to become more upset and more determined to fight the limit. Every time we fail to enforce this limit, we make it harder for ourselves and for them.

When They Find the Loopholes in Your Plan

If there existed some alternative dimension, where things always went according to plan, there would never be flat tires, spam emails, or kids who refused to quietly remain in their bedrooms at night. The world would be free from traffic jams, expired dairy items, and nights spent trying to sleep as kids competed with sharp elbows and knees for our mattress space. Shocking as it may seem, this fairy tale world does not exist... and our kids will test to see if we are truly capable and committed to keeping them from disturbing the nighttime peace.

Perhaps the most predictable thing about parenting is its unpredictability. Every child is different. Some seem born with a peacemaking streak. Others exit the womb smoking cigars and wearing little red boxing gloves. Some are quick to learn. Others require more training. A small number of them respond to techniques just like the experts say they will. Most don't. Many eventually find loopholes in even the best plans.

Sometimes they really drain our energy

Few things are more exhausting than kids who consistently fight the Bedroom Time routine by creating havoc and causing big time problems for others in the home. The noise that comes out of their room wakes baby siblings, alarms close neighbors, causes dogs to howl, and leaves many parents worried. Their persistent refusal to stay in their beds leads to parental exhaustion, lack of intimacy, and thoughts like, "Oh great! What do we do now?"

In Chapter 7 we discussed the *Energy Drain* technique. Does it drain your energy when your little ones absolutely refuse to stay in their beds? Does it drain your energy when they snore in your ear? Do siblings sharing a room drain your volts when they either battle with each other or join forces to wreak nighttime havoc?

Young ones should be expected to replace our energy when they keep us up at night. Energy replacement options include doing extra chores, staying home instead of being taken places they want to go, and hiring their own babysitter so that we can enjoy some relaxing time away.

Liam's parents thought they were ready for the parenting hall of fame. They had successfully conquered the bedtime blues by providing an amazing assortment of choices and by making it very clear to their lovely son and daughter that their doors would remain open only as long as they remained in their rooms. In fact, these parents believed they'd reached the pinnacle of parenting achievement the night Liam decided to sleep standing up. Wedging himself in the corner, sleep won out, and he gently slid into a comfy bundle on the floor. Wise as they were, they remembered the cardinal rule of parenting little ones: Never wake a sleeping child.

A couple of years later, things really changed with the arrival of a new baby brother, Dylan. When this youngest one reached sixteen months of age, he began to share a room with his big brother, Liam. This created a big problem because Dylan was nocturnal. As fate would have it, this basic predisposition soon rubbed off on his older brother. It wasn't long before they were definitely causing problems with the roughhousing, with their almost constant tattling trips to their parents' bedroom:

"Dylan bit me!"

"Liam mean!"

"I'm just drained," Dylan's mother lamented to herself. Then it hit her. "Have an energy drain! That's it. They can replace our energy by paying Mrs. Wilkins to watch them. They can pay with some of their toys. Their dad and I can go on a date without them." The next evening Mrs. Wilkins arrived, wearing a drab housecoat and a headache.

Liam and Dylan's parents empathized, "This is so sad guys. You've been draining our energy by fighting at night and refusing to stay in your room. We're so tired that we need to take a couple hours away to rest. Guys, we pay Mrs. Wilkins when you've been behaving yourself. When you drain our energy, you get to pay her."

Liam was quick to protest, "We can't pay! We don't have money."

With empathy, Dad replied, "That is sad. The only thing I can think of is to pay her with some of your toys. Good luck."

As the words "good" and "luck" came out of Daddy's mouth, daddy, their mother, and their sister Emily left on their outing.

While she wasn't her typical fun self, Mrs. Wilkins was not mean. She was just dull. She was also quite matter of fact as she asked the boys, "How are you planning to pay me for my time?"

Like many other parents across the land, Liam and Dylan's parents discovered that kids tend to get along far better when they understand that failing to do so can result in some sad consequences.

Index

Love and Logic has books and so much more!

CDs
DVDs
One-day Events
Webinars

Visit us at www.loveandlogic.com to see how
Love and Logic can help you have a more rewarding
relationship with the kids in your life.

Sign up for FREE weekly email tips at
www.loveandlogic.com/join